MURDER & MAYHEM IN
PORTLAND
OREGON

MURDER & MAYHEM IN PORTLAND OREGON

JD CHANDLER

THE
History
PRESS

Published by The History Press
Charleston, SC 29403
www.historypress.net

Cover images: *Front*: Portland in the 1870s. *Photograph by Joseph Buchtel. Courtesy of oldoregonphotos.com*; woman shooting competitor, 1902. *Photograph by Walter Bowman. Courtesy of oldoregonphotos.com*; John H. Mitchell. *Courtesy of offbeatoregon.com*; Dong Foot You. *Courtesy of Oregon State Archive, Inmate Record #3035. Back*: Looking toward Mount St. Helens, 1898. *Photograph by Herbert Hale. Courtesy of oldoregonphotos.com*.

First published 2013

ISBN 978.1.5402.0808.8

Library of Congress CIP data applied for

Contents

Acknowledgements

Writing a book is a very lonely business, but paradoxically it can't be done without support and help from friends and acquaintances. The following people have given invaluable help in preparing this book: Dana Beck, Barney Blalock, Steve Chandler, Cari Eisler, Ken Goldstein, Steve Goldstein, Jim Huff, Finn J.D. John, John Klatt, Dina Lingga, Tom Robinson, Leslie Sand, Jake Warren and Nancy Stewart.

In addition, the following institutions or entities, as well as their staffs, have been of immense help: Multnomah County Central Library, especially the John Wilson Special Collections and the Sterling Writer's Room; oldoregonphotos.com; Oregon State Archives; Portland City Archives; Portland Police Museum; and Sellwood-Moreland Improvement League (SMILE).

INTRODUCTION

I've Been Thinking About Murder Lately

E very neighborhood of a city is haunted by the ghosts of the victims of violent crimes. In my neighborhood on a daily basis, I walk past the tavern where a taxi driver picked up his last fare before being killed for the cash he had collected that night. I walk past several apartment buildings where women—from Gwen Ponsson in 1942 to Nikayla Powell in 2012—have been killed by lovers or other strangers. I walk past the dumpster where the body of a seven-year-old boy was found thirty years ago and the bowling alley where an employee was shot to death on my last birthday. My neighborhood is not more violent than any of the other neighborhoods in Portland, or any other American city, but it is haunted by countless murder victims. It is probably the most common experience among city dwellers to know about a murder in the neighborhood or to know someone who has been murdered.

No one is immune. Homicide and other violent crimes happen to everyone regardless of gender, ethnicity, occupation, wealth (or its lack) or any other category. A homicide can and does happen to anyone at any time. That's why it makes such an interesting study. By looking at who has been killed and who has done the killing, we learn about how people lived and died. Sometimes a murder investigation brings to light things that are not remembered anywhere else. By studying the history of murder in a city, we get a glimpse into the lives of its residents, the things they thought about and the problems they faced. By looking at the history of a murder investigation, we learn a lot about the relationship between the citizens and the police force. We learn how the police force and the methods its officers use to enforce the law have changed. Ironically, the study of the history of murder can make the history of a city come alive.

Portland, besides being my favorite city, is a good example of the urban development of the American West. Founded by merchants and real estate developers, Portland has been seen as a city since its first settlement in the 1840s, when it was just a few cabins in an area known as "the Clearing." The city was incorporated in 1851, and its first recorded murder occurred just a few weeks later. Portland is not a particularly violent city; in comparison to other American cities, it has always had a modest homicide rate. As the population grew, the murder rate grew with it, reaching a peak in the 1980s and gradually settling into a steady level. Portland's police department has not always been good at solving murders; in fact, sometimes it hasn't even bothered to investigate, but every year skills and technology develop in ways that make it easier to catch killers.

In this book, I have an opportunity to share my obsession with the history of my favorite city and its murders. I hope it will help the history of Portland come alive for my readers. I hope it will give you a glimpse into the dark hearts of the killers and the lost lives of the victims. Most importantly, I hope it will help all of us to remember the people who have come before and lost their lives to the violence of city life. With that in mind, I dedicate this book to the victims of murder, and I hope it will let them live in history and in our memories.

Pioneer Murder, 1858

Just six months after Oregon became a state, Multnomah County executed its first murderer. Danforth Balch's crime, a public shooting in broad daylight, was long remembered as Portland's first murder, but it really wasn't. That dubious honor goes to a man named Cook, who was shot to death at a saloon on Front Street, now Naito Parkway, on April 1, 1851, about six weeks after the city was incorporated. Cook, who was twenty at the time of his death, was killed by William Keene (or Kean) from Missouri. The two men argued in the bar and then shot it out in Wild West fashion. Portland was in Washington County in those days, so Keene was tried in Hillsboro, convicted of manslaughter and sentenced to six months.

The murder of Mortimer Stump by Danforth Balch, while not the first murder in Portland, is the first well-documented case of homicide. It took place on the Stephen's ferry at the Westside Stark Street landing on November 18, 1858. Stump was a former employee of Balch, who owned a land grant northwest of Captain Couch's grant, in the west hills of Portland. Stump, whose family lived in East Portland, a separate city in those days, worked on Balch's farm and lived in the Balch home for a few years. In the process, he fell in love with Balch's oldest daughter, Anna. When she was sixteen, Stump went to her father and asked for permission to marry the girl.

Danforth Balch, born in Massachusetts in 1811, came west from Iowa in 1848 and settled on a land grant near Guilds Lake in a neighborhood that became known as Willamette Heights. Balch Creek, which runs through Macleay Park and the Pittock Bird Sanctuary and was once a major logging stream feeding the mills on Portland's waterfront, is on land that once belonged to Danforth Balch. Balch had little education, "two or three

Before 1888, the only way across the Willamette to the separate city of East Portland was the Stark Street Ferry, which landed at the foot of Stark Street, in the background of this photo. In 1858, the ferry became the scene of one of Portland's first murders. *Photograph by Joseph Buchtel. Courtesy of oldoregonphotos.com.*

seasons" according to his statement published after his execution, but by 1858, he had a prosperous farm about a mile and a half from Portland and a large family. The thought of his oldest daughter marrying at sixteen seems to have caused him to become unhinged. He fired Stump, threatened to kill him if he came around his daughter and chased him off his land.

Stump's love for the young woman was not unrequited; she eloped with him a few weeks later. The lovers went to Vancouver, where they were married, and they spent a few more weeks on honeymoon somewhere nearby. According to Danforth Balch's final statement, he hardly ate or slept after his daughter left, and he didn't remember much of what he did during that time. The rumor was that it was alcohol that made Balch forget. Whatever it was, Balch was in a bad mood on November 18 when he saw the Stumps near the corner of Stark and Front Streets.

Mortimer Stump and his bride, accompanied by his parents, had just finished buying furniture for their new house in East Portland. They loaded their furniture on a wagon and boarded the Stark Street ferry to cross to

Danforth Balch shot his son-in-law, Mortimer Stump, to death in front of several witnesses and became the first man to be executed by Multnomah County in 1859. The crime had become legendary by the time this drawing ran in the *Oregonian* in 1920. *Courtesy of the* Oregonian, *Oregonian Historical Archive, Multnomah County Library, Portland, Oregon.*

their new home. Danforth Balch was standing in front of Starr's tin shop on the corner when the wagon went by. Harsh words were exchanged between Balch and the elder Stump. According to Balch's statement, Stump's father said, "You're making a big deal about an ordinary little bitch." Enraged by the comment, Balch followed the party and caught sight of his daughter as she boarded the ferry. He said that he followed the wagon onto the ferry to get his daughter back and that he had his shotgun only because he had heard that Mortimer Stump had promised to "beat him to the ground." Balch claimed that it was an accident that the gun went off, twice, but in his enraged and possibly drunken state, it would have been more of an accident if it *hadn't* gone off. Mortimer Stump took two barrels of buckshot in the face and upper chest. He died instantly. The Balch case, as it came to be known, played an important role in the careers of two notorious Portlanders: James Lappeus and John H. Mitchell.

Lappeus came west with a regiment of New York Volunteers during the Mexican-American War in 1847 and then stayed in California to gamble and prey on gold rushers. Lappeus became a notorious "black leg" gambler and was involved with the gang known as the Hounds, which inspired the Sacramento Vigilante Committee to lynch several members of the gang. Coming north when things got too hot in California, Lappeus was soon part owner of the finest gambling establishment in Portland, the Oro Fino Theater and Gem Saloon. Lappeus was elected town marshal shortly after the Stump murder. At the time Lappeus took office, Balch had escaped from the city jail and

James Lappeus, Portland's first career police officer. He had a long career on both sides of the law. *Courtesy of the Portland Police Historical Society.*

had been at large for some time. Lappeus soon tracked the fugitive down; he was camping on his own land in what is now Forest Park. Lappeus allegedly offered to "leave the door open again" if Balch would pay $1,000 (more than $25,000 in 2013). Although nothing came of the offer, if it occurred, the rumor haunted Lappeus's career as town marshal and eventually police chief, contributing to its end in 1883.

John H. Mitchell, born John Mitchell Hipple in 1835 in Pennsylvania, started his career as a schoolteacher in his home state. In 1857, a sexual affair with a fifteen-year-old student forced him to resign his teaching position and marry the girl. He decided to go into the practice of law, but soon he embezzled $4,000 (more than $95,000 in 2013) from his employer, which he later paid back, and abandoned his young bride to go to California with his mistress, Maria Brinker. In 1860, he grew bored with Brinker, left for Oregon without her and changed his name, switching the order of his middle and last names. Soon he had a law practice and a new wife, although he hadn't bothered to divorce the first one.

John H. Mitchell shortly before he was elected to the U.S. Senate. He was a bigamist and an embezzler, and he was accused of defrauding the Balch family of their land after Danforth Balch was executed. His successful defense was that the statute of limitations had expired. *Courtesy of offbeatoregon.com.*

Sharp men with flexible ethics have always prospered in Portland, and Mitchell was no exception. Mary Jane Balch, the killer's widow who had eight little children to support, turned to lawyer Mitchell for help. Mitchell, as if trying out for the part of villain in a melodrama, defrauded the family of all of their land, which was divvied up with some influential people, such as Henry Pittock of the *Oregonian*. Mitchell was soon serving his first term in the Senate, after the Ethics Committee ruled that his conduct before entering the Senate, such as embezzlement and bigamy, were not relevant.

When the Balch children came of age and tried to get their land back, Mitchell pled that the statute of limitations had expired, and he was not tried. It did raise embarrassing issues during his campaigns for Senate and contributed to the debacle that left one of Oregon's Senate seats vacant in 1896. Mitchell was never one to let a little thing like ethics get in the way of his career, and he was reelected to the Senate in 1900. An even bigger land swindle, involving thousands of acres of timber land in the Cascades, came to light in 1903, and in 1905, Mitchell was indicted for fraud and conspiracy and convicted by the Senate. Before he could be sentenced for his crimes, Mitchell, who was seventy years old, died from complications of a tooth extraction in Portland.

A little less than a year after Mortimer Stump's murder, the age of public execution began in Portland when Danforth Balch was hanged in the stockade just south of the city jail on Alder Street between Front and First Streets. Public execution lasted in Portland from 1859 to 1903, but it was not a common occurrence. Balch's execution drew a crowd of about six hundred people (most of them from outside of Portland), including the entire Stump family with Anna Balch Stump, who wanted to see her father hang for killing her husband. After that, hangings, often clumped together to execute three or four criminals at a time, drew much bigger crowds. One of the biggest crowds, estimated at nearly four thousand people, gathered for the hanging of Archie Brown and James Johnson on March 10, 1879, nearly twenty years after the execution of Balch.

Mayhem on Morrison Street, 1878

The violence of the Old West that is pervasively portrayed in the movies and popular literature is mostly a myth. The truth is that western cities, such as Portland, became *more* violent the farther they got from pioneer days. The two most common forms of murder in the nineteenth century, as in the twentieth and twenty-first, were killings that arose out of domestic disputes, such as the murder of Mortimer Stump, and alcohol-related violence, such as Portland's first recorded murder, the shooting of Cook. The third most common motive for murder is robbery. The excitement and public uproar that accompanied the shooting of Louis Joseph, a fourteen-year-old boy, during a violent armed robbery in downtown Portland illustrates how rare these kinds of crimes were at that time. The public execution of two of the robbers in 1879 was the most attended execution ever held in Portland and required military occupation of the area around the Multnomah County Courthouse.

By 1878, Portland was a bustling metropolis, collecting and distributing ore, beef, wool and wheat from the Columbia and Snake River country, as well as fruit, hops and lumber from the Willamette Valley. These commodities collected in Portland for transport to the rest of the world; manufactured goods, clothing and other necessities were made in Portland or came in from San Francisco for distribution to the countryside. This brisk business left a good residue of money in Portland that was gathered up by the merchants, sea captains and real estate speculators who are now revered as the fathers of the city. Very little of this money remained in the hands of working people, and the little that did was absorbed by the saloons, *bagnios* and opium dens of the waterfront and the North End in the area that is now known as Old

Flood, fire and financial panic shaped Portland in the 1870s, but the city continued to grow and prosper. *Photographed by Joseph Buchtel. Courtesy of oldoregonphotos.com.*

Town. Most of the working people in Portland, a disproportionate number of whom were single men, lived a boom or bust lifestyle, and pawnshops did a brisk business.

Portland's growing economy was stimulated by business in the harbor. Prosperity attracted criminals from out of state. *Photograph by Joseph Buchtel. Courtesy of oldoregonphotos.com.*

Walter O'Shea was a prosperous pawnbroker with a shop on the south side of Washington Street between First and Second, an area that is now a parking lot and the approach to the Morrison Bridge. In 1878, it was a busy corner, with several shops and stores of various kinds. Business was good. On Monday, August 19, O'Shea had more than $8,000 (nearly $180,000 in 2013) in his safe, but he had removed most of it, and the next day, he probably only had about $1,000 cash in the shop. Shortly after he opened on Tuesday, two men, known as Archie Brown and James Johnson, entered the store and said that they wanted to buy blankets. Sixteen-year-old Charles Schwartz (aka Joseph Swoards) came in behind them. Brown and Johnson dickered with O'Shea over the blankets. When Schwartz came in, Johnson admonished him to close the door. "Why?" asked the young man. "We don't want anyone to see," Johnson replied.

"Terrible Tragedy: Assault, Robbery and Murder"
Oregonian, August 21, 1878

The men agreed on a price, and Johnson offered cash for the blankets. O'Shea squatted down behind the counter to open his safe and get change. Brown picked up a convenient iron bar and brained O'Shea with three vicious blows. The first blow, to the top of O'Shea's head, opened a deep wound in his scalp, exposing the skull. The second and third blows aimed at the back of O'Shea's head were not as strong, but they rendered him unconscious. Johnson sprang to the door, locked it and then scooped the jewelry from the window displays, stuffing them into a handy valise. Brown grabbed the cash from the safe and took the valise from Johnson.

Ed Miller and Lee Backenstos, two pioneer layabouts in their early twenties, were standing on the sidewalk across the street from O'Shea's. Backenstos, one of the first white men born in Oregon, was the son of a military officer who had been stationed at Fort Vancouver. He would later be a pioneer morphine addict. Miller's forte would be forgery. In 1878, they watched the three men enter the pawnshop and then saw Johnson lock the door and grab jewelry from the window. Looking down the street, they spotted Constable Sprague and fireman W.W. Sweeny talking on the corner. Alerted to the robbery in progress, the two unarmed men approached the pawnshop. Sprague covered the front, while Sweeny attempted to get around to the back.

Sweeny had to climb up to the roof to see into the backyard. As he reached the roof, he heard shattering glass and saw the robbers break through a window and climb the fence into the adjoining yard. Brown brandished a pistol as the men walked boldly through the Lewis and Strauss store and out onto the sidewalk of First Street. Sweeny motioned to Sprague, letting him know which way the men were going, and Sprague gave chase.

The men turned west on Alder Street, with Sprague in pursuit. Johnson turned back and warned the unarmed officer, but he continued his pursuit. The valise that Brown was carrying was heavy, and he had trouble keeping up with the other two running men. As they reached the corner of Third and Alder, Brown was heard to say, "Damn it let's make a stand right here; I've run just as far as I'm going to go." Johnson looked back and saw Sprague getting close. He said, "Give it to him."

Johnson and Schwartz kept running. Brown turned, pointed his navy pistol at Sprague and fired. Just as Brown fired, Sprague bent down to pick up a rock to throw at the robber. Louis Joseph, fourteen, who had been working at his father's glazier shop on Alder Street, came out of the store to see what the commotion was about. The bullet intended for Sprague struck the boy in the center of his chest, and he died instantly. Brown fired once more, and Sprague ducked behind a tree to avoid being shot. The three robbers jumped into a horse-drawn wagon in front of the Weeks and Morgan Grocery Store and raced from town, heading west on Morrison Street. They abandoned the wagon at Fifteenth Street. Brown, who had become frustrated with the heavy valise full of coins and jewelry, removed the coins and distributed them among his partners during the wagon ride. He had also rifled the jewelry, keeping the most valuable and smallest items, such as a diamond set valued at over $1,000 and several gold watches, before discarding the valise and much of the jewelry in the backyard of a residence. The three men disappeared into the woods of Washington Park, then known as City Park.

Within minutes of the shots, hundreds of people, many of them armed, had poured into the streets of downtown. Police Chief Lucerne Besser personally took control of the investigation and sent eight armed officers in pursuit of the robbers. Within an hour, more than fifty well-armed volunteers had joined the hunt, and guards were posted on all routes in and out of the city. Even Jim Turk, who would soon become a dominant force in the crimping trade, got into the act, bringing in two men he arrested when he became suspicious of the $100 cash he found on them. The two men were quickly released by the police, but it would be surprising if Turk didn't end up with their money somehow.

Some historians have questioned the pervasiveness of gun ownership in the nineteenth-century West, but there is plenty of evidence that most, if not all, Portlanders owned guns. Two days after the robbery at O'Shea's, the *Oregonian* reported on a series of burglaries on the remote east side of the Willamette. In every reported case, the burglars were foiled when homeowners opened fire with shotguns or handguns. These reports are common in the *Oregonian* through the 1870s and 1880s. Portlanders believed in citizen participation in law enforcement. When violent crime threatened the community, especially when it involved children, armed posses were formed to support, and sometimes coerce, the police in their investigations. In the case of O'Shea's robbers, a reward of $250 ($5,500 in 2013), posted within an hour of the robbery, stimulated the citizen response. Unarmed crowds, numbering more than one hundred, continued to surround the city jail in the interest of "seeing justice done" if any suspects were located.

Fortunately, no suspects were caught that day or the next. There was a large public funeral for the Joseph boy, and a crowd of supporters accompanied his body to Beth Israel Cemetery on Taylor's Ferry Road south of town. Public sentiment ran high, but with no suspects, it began to cool. Some merchants were willing to commercialize on public feeling by using the crime in their advertising. After the funeral, the crowd downtown began to disperse.

"Next to the Robbery, the Greatest Excitement in Town Is the Low Prices at the C.O.D. Grocery"
Oregonian, ad, August 21, 1878

At about 11:00 p.m. that night, Special Officer Gwynne and another man were scouting the lonely road north of town along the Willamette on the way to Linnton. Near the Terminus Saloon, a notorious dive that had already witnessed a fatal shooting that summer, the two hunters startled a group of three men. Two of them ran off in different directions and got away; Charles Schwartz was captured and returned to Portland. Schwartz, sixteen years old, had arrived in Portland a few weeks before on a ship from Philadelphia. A runaway with no money or prospects, Schwartz was picked up by two men who lived in a hotel in the North End. "Taking a fancy" to the boy, the two men told him that he was too good to work and that he should stick with them. They even paid his board at the hotel while they cased the city looking for a target to rob, although Schwartz said that he thought they were looking for work.

The two men were Eugene Avery, twenty-four, of Waterton, Wisconsin, known by his alias Archie Brown, and a man called James Johnson, who was also in his early twenties (his real name was never revealed). Avery had migrated west from his impoverished family farm at the age of sixteen, arriving in Sacramento in 1870. Avery worked as a farm laborer and soon drifted into petty crime. He served two terms in San Quentin Penitentiary for theft. During his second incarceration, he made the acquaintance of James Johnson. Johnson was said to be the black sheep of a socially prominent San Francisco family and served a long term in San Quentin for armed robbery. Upon his release from prison in 1878, Avery bummed around the San Jose area looking for work and then decided to buy a cheap fare to Portland to see if the grass was greener. Avery claimed that it was a coincidence that he ran into Johnson in a North End dive in Portland, but the two jailbirds soon got together and were sharing a boy and planning a crime.

Avery followed the river, hiding during the daytime and traveling at night. He was ragged, hungry and discouraged when he reached the Cain farm eleven miles west of Portland. Concealing the watches and cash that he still carried from the robbery, Avery told the family that he was Archie Brown and asked if he could stay on the farm a few days. It was harvest time, and there was plenty of work to be done, so John Cain agreed to rent a bed to the stranger. Avery took a few days to recover from his hungry trek and then stayed away from the farm during the day, pretending to look for work but actually hiding in the woods. After four days, Cain and his daughter were highly suspicious of the young man, and soon Cain arrested him and took him to Portland as one of O'Shea's robbers.

Johnson, who had gone south when Schwartz was captured, made his way over the West Hills and was finally arrested in October 1878 in Los Angeles, where he was trying to sell the diamond set from O'Shea's. He was returned to Portland on October 29, 1878, quickly convicted of first-degree murder and sentenced to death. Avery was also sentenced to death. Schwartz, under the name of Joseph Swoards, was convicted of second-degree murder and sentenced to life, although both Johnson and Avery said that he had nothing at all to do with the robbery and had been surprised by it. Schwartz died of consumption in prison in 1883.

In the public mind, the execution of Johnson and Avery in March 1879 was one of the great events of the decade. People began to gather around the Multnomah County Courthouse before dawn on the day of the execution. Nearly four thousand people gathered on the streets that morning to witness the hanging. A large number of Chinese, as many as eight hundred, also attended the execution. They were curious because a Chinese killer, Ah Lee, was scheduled to hang later that year. The city was taking no chances on the large crowd disrupting the proceedings. Cannons were stationed at the corners of the courthouse, and soldiers of the Emmett Guard, City Rifles, Portland Battery and the Washington Guards assembled around the stockade. The militia soldiers assembled at 8:00 a.m., their bayonets glittering in the pale early spring sunlight. By noon, guards were stationed at all of the street corners in the neighborhood.

"JOHNSON AND BROWN: EXPIATION OF THEIR CRIME UPON THE GALLOWS—THEIR LAST FLEETING HOURS"
Oregonian, March 10, 1879

The scaffold stood inside a stockade of tall wooden planks that enclosed the block to the south of the courthouse, where city hall now stands. The crowd filled the yard to overflowing, and many people pressed against the fence, peering through knotholes. The hanging was scheduled for 1:00 p.m., but the prisoners didn't emerge from their cells until 1:40 p.m. The two condemned men were taken to the gallows, and Sheriff Ben L. Norden read the death warrant before asking the prisoners if they had anything to say. Johnson answered, "Nothing." Avery took full advantage of the opportunity. Jumping onto the trapdoor, he denounced the judge who condemned him for prejudice, and then he began a long recitation of the details of his life and the crimes he had committed.

Sheriff Norden was lenient, allowing Brown to talk and sing songs for nearly half an hour. Johnson finally snapped, "Brown, I wish you would get to the point. This suspense is terrible for me." Avery finished up with a religious appeal and a plea for people to heed his example and avoid crime. Then the men were hanged.

The year 1879 was a busy one on the scaffold. In addition to Johnson and Brown, Ah Lee, a Portland Chinese man; Jackson Grant, a "Digger" (probably Modoc) Indian; and three Alaskan Indians were executed in Portland that year. Public hangings remained a fixture of Portland life until the state took control of executions in 1903. The last public execution in Portland was that of A.L. Belding, who killed his wife, her mother and another man on June 11, 1902. The trial was conducted quickly, and the execution was scheduled just days before the new law went into effect on June 1, 1903.

The Court of Death, 1881

I t was a raw and blustery morning on Friday, November 25, 1881, as two men walked along the north waterfront toward the Nicolai Planing Mill, where they worked. The waterfront near the foot of Everett Street was a muddy field full of debris, dominated by lumber mills and the "boneyard," where disabled steamboats were stored. Derelict boats were moored in the shallow water or beached in the mud. The two men were startled to see two naked human legs waving from the shallow water just offshore. Bodies in the Willamette were not unusual. It is a big river, and it was routine for people to fall from boats or even to commit suicide by jumping into the river. Some bodies from farther up river would wash ashore in Portland as well. The two millworkers hurried on to their work at Second and Everett Streets. When they arrived, they reported the floater to the foreman.

Coroner John Garnold had to use a small rowboat to pull the corpse out of the river. The ankles were bound together with a piece of wire, and Garnold struggled for a while before realizing that a rope tied around the corpse's neck was attached to a hundred-pound stone. Finally getting the body to shore, he found that it was a man in his early fifties. The man was wearing only his shirt, collar and tie. The only identifying marks were semicircular scars on each eyebrow and a trimmed gray mustache and chin beard. The corpse had been in the water for a few weeks and had evidently been thrown overboard from a small boat, judging from its position in the river. The water had been unusually low that fall; the body might never have been discovered. Garnold put the decaying body on display at the city morgue, and many people viewed it, but none identified the dead man.

By the 1880s, Portland had become the second-largest city on the West Coast. Workers from all over Oregon and Washington came to Portland when they needed a dentist or when they wanted to have a good time. *Photograph by Isaac Davidson. Courtesy of oldoregonphotos.com.*

A young prostitute called Dolly Adams viewed the body and took great interest in the things that had been found with it. Tangled in the victim's shirt was a small white towel. Dolly hurried home to the "boardinghouse" where she lived in Portland's Tenderloin district and shared the news. Carrie Bradley, the twenty-eight-year-old woman who employed four prostitutes in her *bagnio*, was very interested. That afternoon, she gathered all the towels in the house and burned them in the parlor stove.

The body remained on display for several days, and then someone said that they thought it might be a man named Andrews. Garnold probably wanted to get the ripe corpse out of his morgue, so he buried it in the potter's field and let it go at that. Police Chief James Lappeus was involved in the political infighting with city council member Lucerne Besser that would soon end his long career on both sides of the law. According to Officer John J. Flynn, Lappeus accepted $500 ($11,000 in 2013) from Carrie Bradley to allow her and her accomplices to skip town before they could be connected with the murder. Constable Sam Simmons, though, was an ambitious young cop intent on making a name for himself. He refused to let the unidentified man rest in peace.

The body had been badly beaten either shortly before or shortly after death, but the two semicircular scars on the man's eyebrows seemed to be very old. Simmons decided that these scars were the key to the man's identity.

On November 25, 1881, two millworkers on their way to work at the Nicolai Brothers' Mill were startled to see two legs waving from the river not far from where this photo was taken. *Photograph by Edward Partridge. Courtesy of oldoregonphotos.com.*

Assuming that the dead man had been a visitor to town, Simmons checked every hotel, asking the staff about a man with scars on his head. Soon he discovered that James Nelson Brown from Freeport, Washington, had been staying in the National Hotel in October.

Brown had worked for several years as a timber spotter in Freeport, just across the Columbia River from Clatskanie, Oregon. In the fall of 1881, he decided to retire and sold his land, heading for Portland on a spree with $4,000 ($89,000 in 2013) in his pocket. Arriving in Portland, he checked into the National Hotel on Front Street at Yamhill, just blocks from the Tenderloin, an area of open prostitution surrounded by saloons. He began to frequent saloons and *bagnios*, and he gambled and stayed drunk for days.

In 1881, prostitution wasn't legal, but it was not considered a serious offense and was often tolerated. In the 1880 census, fifty-eight women listed their occupations as prostitute; almost every one of them lived on the square block bounded by Third and Fourth Streets and Yamhill and Taylor Streets. This is the block known as the Tenderloin to contemporaries, but the *Oregonian* commonly called it the "Court of Death." In 1881, it consisted of two or three large houses, referred to as "boardinghouses" or *bagnios*. The rest of the block was made up of small cottages known as cribs, just large enough for a bed, a washstand and a window seat where women could sit to entice customers. Some of the girls decorated their cribs nicely and put in gardens or cultivated trellises of ivy. One section was devoted to upscale French courtesans.

Carrie Bradley kept the house that stood on the southwest corner of Third and Yamhill. In the 1880 census, she listed her occupation as "Boarding House Keeper" and had four boarders: Fay Williams, twenty-one; Mollie Moss, fifteen; Molly Thompson, nineteen; and Belle Boyd, twenty-one. All four women were listed as prostitutes. There were also two Chinese men who lived in the house as servants (and probably muscle). The women's names were very changeable; by 1881, each of them was using a different name. The young woman known as Belle Boyd was

J. Nelson Brown, a timber spotter from Freeport, Washington Territory, came to Portland with $4,000 for a spree. No one knows what happened to his money. *Courtesy of the Oregonian,* Oregonian Historical Archive, Multnomah County Library, Portland, Oregon.

known as Dolly Adams one year later, although we may never know her real name. Belle Boyd was the name of a famous Confederate spy of the Civil War; Dolly Adams was a performer known as the "Water Queen," famous for her swimming act.

One night in October, Brown ventured into Carrie Bradley's place. Bradley, at twenty-eight years old, did not actively work as a prostitute by this time. She came to Portland in 1877, probably from New York by way of San Francisco. She was an attractive woman, but she had a mean temper and a violent streak. For the previous two years, she had been in a relationship with Charley Hamilton, a well-known saloon brawler, and there had been more than one violent altercation at her *bagnio*, including one in June 1881 in which she had Hamilton arrested for hitting her and setting the place on fire. She ruled her "girls" with an iron hand, and they were always a little afraid of her. Early that year, a young man fresh out of the Oregon State Penitentiary, Pete Sullivan, had become infatuated with Molly Flippen (Thompson)

Carrie Bradley ran a *bagnio* in Portland's Tenderloin. She had a violent streak and ruled her girls with an iron hand. *Courtesy of the* Oregonian, *Oregonian Historical Archive, Multnomah County Library, Portland, Oregon.*

and began to hang around Bradley's place. Carrie took a liking to him and asked him to move in. She soon began to train him as a procurer.

Bradley knew how to put on a great show. Customers would spend time in the parlor, where Professor Otto Jordan played piano and carefully minded his own business. Drinking was encouraged, as was chloroform use, before going upstairs with your chosen girl. Chloroform abuse is very dangerous, but it was undergoing a bit of a fad in 1881. Men would rub drops of chloroform into their mustache and women into their upper lip, and the fumes would make them dizzy or a little sick. It was a popular pastime at Bradley's. Laudanum, a tincture of opium in alcohol, was another popular drug at Bradley's, used by the prostitutes habitually and by customers occasionally. Bradley had her own use for laudanum as well; when Sullivan would come across a mark with money, he would bring him back to Bradley's for a party. She would put laudanum into his drink, and he would pass out, waking up, sometimes in another part of town, to find his money gone.

Brown didn't have a lot of money on him the night he spent with Dolly Adams. The next day, he had her arrested and charged with stealing $6 from him while he slept. It isn't clear what happened to the $4,000 Brown came to town with, although it is possible that he had blown most of it on his spree by this time. He was angry about the robbery, though—angry enough that he insisted on pressing charges and seeing Dolly in jail.

The Tenderloin was not in the North End, where more respectable Portlanders preferred to keep their rowdy entertainment. Prostitution was tolerated outside the North End, in places like Della Burris's house on Park Street or Madame Lida Fanshaw's place one block from the prestigious Arlington Club, but only if it was discreet. Carrie Bradley was not discreet, and worse, the Court of Death was only a few blocks away from a cluster of churches in the "respectable" part of town. Multnomah County district attorney John F. Caples saw Bradley's angry customer as a way to put pressure on Bradley and maybe even get her out of town. He already had four or five other charges pending against her and thought with Brown's testimony he might be able to finally shut her down. Brown agreed to testify against Bradley and even went so far as to pay a twenty-five-dollar bond to guarantee his appearance in court.

Multnomah County district attorney John F. Caples saw a chance to put more pressure on Carrie Bradley as part of his campaign to move prostitution out of the Tenderloin. *Courtesy of the* Oregonian, *Oregonian Historical Archive, Multnomah County Library, Portland, Oregon.*

Brown wasn't completely out of money; over the next few days, he was seen drinking and gambling with friends around town as usual. Carrie Bradley was seriously angry though. She told Sullivan to do whatever was necessary to get Brown back to her place. Sullivan spent several days following Brown from saloon to saloon but was not able to get him alone until one night late in October 1881. Brown was having a drink at Chauncey Dale's Grotto Saloon on Morrison between First and Second. Brown was alone, so Sullivan and his young sidekick, Asa "Ace" Nisonger, joined him. Brown was friendly, and Sullivan was good at his job, but when he mentioned going to Bradley's, Brown said he didn't want anything to do with the place. Sullivan signaled Ace to go get Carrie.

Carrie Bradley and Dolly Adams showed up a little while later. When they came in, Brown said to Sullivan, "That's the girl I had arrested." Carrie turned to him and said, "Is that you, Mr. Brown?" She was all smiles and charm as she apologized for the trouble they had experienced, and soon they were drinking happily together. Sullivan and Brown even broke into song more than once, until Chauncey Dale warned them to keep the noise down.

Carrie said that they could sing and dance all they wanted at her place. Brown said that he didn't want to go back to that den of thieves, but Bradley batted her eyes at him and said, "But tonight you go with me."

Bradley was a charming and sexy woman, and Brown was pretty drunk, so soon he found himself in her comfortable parlor. Carrie ordered Professor Jordan to play a lively tune. Jordan noticed that Brown was "tight" when they came in, and Sullivan and Brown danced around a bit before settling on the lounge. Fay Cushing saw Carrie putting morphine into Brown's drink and said, "Miss Carrie, don't do that." Brown snapped at her, "Mind your own business; you always have too much to say around this house, and if you don't like it you know what you can do." Brown had several drinks laced with morphine. Bradley asked Ace if he had any chloroform, but he was out, so she gave him one dollar and sent him to the drugstore for more.

Brown was a tough man and a hard drinker. By 1:00 a.m., he had consumed a huge amount of brandy and an unknown amount of morphine. It was no wonder that he had to be carried upstairs and put into Sullivan's bed. Dolly and Carrie stripped him of his clothes but for some reason left his shirt and collar on. Then Carrie took a small white towel and saturated it with chloroform, tying it around Brown's nose and mouth. They left him alone in the bed and closed the door. Carrie Bradley took Dolly aside in the hall and told her that it was going to cost $150 ($3,400 in 2013) to get Brown out of the way, and since it was her fault, it was money that she owed. Dolly agreed and gave her $90, saying that she would owe her the rest.

"DRUGGED TO DEATH: IDENTITY OF THE CORPSE FOUND NEAR WEIDLER'S MILL"
Oregonian, February 12, 1882

Sullivan and Ace Nisonger went out and gambled until about 3:00 a.m. When they got home, Ace went to Fay Cushing's room; Sullivan slept with Carrie Bradley. At about 9:00 a.m., Dolly Adams knocked on Bradley's door. "He's dead," she said. Sullivan rushed to his room and found Brown, whose face had turned deep purple, dead in the bed. Morphine and chloroform is a deadly mixture; morphine slows the breathing, decreasing oxygen intake, and chloroform replaces oxygen. Brown suffocated without gaining consciousness.

A few minutes later, Carrie Bradley burst into the room wearing a pair of brass knuckles that Charley Hamilton had made to fit her hand.

"You two are in this as deep as me," she said. "You have to help me get rid of him." She then turned to the corpse on the bed and vented her anger by beating it with the brass knuckles. Sullivan and Adams got the message. When Carrie had tired herself out, she ordered Sullivan to take the body downstairs to the basement, and she sent Dolly Adams out to find Charley Hamilton. When the other members of the household woke up, Carrie told them that she wasn't feeling well and sent them to work at the White House, south of town on Macadam Road, while she kept her house closed up.

Hamilton, with Tommy Wilson, a gambler's apprentice who would become one of the most famous gamblers in town by the end of the century, soon arrived and found Sullivan trying to dig a grave in the unfinished basement with a fireplace shovel. Bradley said that she wanted a six-foot-deep grave, but Sullivan was barely able to scratch out a few feet before covering the body with dirt. Hamilton was disgusted and sent Wilson out to get a big trunk and hire a buggy. He had a plan.

Under cover of darkness that night, Hamilton, Sullivan and a young hack driver named John A. Mahone moved the body, dropping the trunk twice along the way and injuring Hamilton's foot in the process. They finally reached the waterfront and disposed of the corpse. That night was a macabre comedy of errors as the drug addicts worked ineptly to dispose of the corpse only to have it found grotesquely sticking out of the water a few weeks later.

The trials that followed were a sensation. Most of the defendants had skipped town and were arrested in San Francisco. John Mahone testified for the prosecution and was not charged. Charley Hamilton was never seen again. There were rumors of him visiting Portland, but nothing was confirmed. There was also a rumor that he had been hanged by Mexican authorities. It would make sense that someone hanged Charley Hamilton. Pete Sullivan pled guilty and served four years in the Oregon State Penitentiary.

Carrie Bradley accused Dolly Adams of being the killer, but no one believed her. Adams testified for the state and only served a short time in jail; she undoubtedly changed her name again when she was released. Bradley was convicted of manslaughter and sentenced to twelve years. She was released after five years and set up a new *bagnio* in Sisson, California. Sisson would later change its name to Mount Shasta. Pete Sullivan was arrested in San Francisco in 1894 for enticing young women into prostitution. He was still plying his old trade as procurer for Bradley's new place. Sullivan was sentenced to five years at San Quentin. Sullivan's conviction and sentence

Ex–police chief Lucerne Besser was a city council member in 1882. He was involved in a corrupt plot to take control of the police department and engineered the firing of Chief Lappeus. *Courtesy of Portland Police Historical Society.*

were too much for Carrie Bradley. She shot herself shortly after Sullivan went to prison.

The murder trial had serious political repercussions. Both of Bradley's defense attorneys were charged with attempting to influence the jury. W. Scott Beebe, one of the defense attorneys, was a partisan of Lucerne Besser. The charges against him and O.P. Mason were most likely politically motivated, and they don't seem to have resulted in any type of discipline. Beebe would not be a stranger to scandal, though. He specialized in criminal defense and probate law, and he often seems to have mixed the two. In one probate case in 1890, one of the parties involved shot the other but only wounded him. In 1896, Beebe was party to a nasty divorce in which his wife accused him of morphine addiction, financial impropriety and insanity. There was evidence for all of her charges.

Police Chief James Lappeus was a political victim of the Bradley case as well. Lappeus—who had been an outlaw, a law-flaunting gambler, Portland town marshal and Portland's first police chief—was charged with malfeasance in the handling of the Bradley case, and while he was on trial for the charges, the old issue of bribery in the Balch case resurfaced. It was the end for Lappeus, and he soon retired from police work. The political shenanigans of Lappeus and Besser hampered District Attorney Caples's campaign to move prostitution out of the Tenderloin, even with all the publicity of Bradley's trial. In 1885, another murder in the Court of Death signaled the end of open prostitution in the Tenderloin.

On December 21, 1885, an attractive and cultured French courtesan called Emma Merlotin (real name Ana Decoz) was hacked to death with a hatchet in her crib. Merlotin was a popular young woman, and her death created great excitement. Rumors flew that she had been murdered by one

This lithograph from *West Shore* magazine was the face that Portland wanted to present to the world in the 1880s. The truth was a little darker. *Courtesy of oldoregonphotos.com.*

of her clients, a wealthy young man from an influential family. It is possible that the rumors were correct because the police investigation consisted of an inept roundup of usual suspects and little else. The *Portland Daily News* milked the crime for a few days' worth of stories, but the *Oregonian* virtually ignored it. The death of Merlotin, which is hauntingly similar to the case of Helen Jewett in New York City nearly fifty years earlier, soon became one of Portland's most enduring unsolved mysteries.

The second lurid murder in the Tenderloin in just a few years increased public pressure to move the prostitutes out. By the end of the decade, they had quietly relocated to the North End, where they didn't have to be seen by respectable people, and Portland's Tenderloin soon faded from public memory.

The Girl in the Strawberry Patch, 1892

The year 1892 was a good one for Portland. The year before, the city had merged with East Portland and Albina (North Portland) to create the largest city in the Pacific Northwest. Business was booming, and the depression that would hit in the spring of 1893 was still in the future. Since the opening of the Morrison Bridge in 1887, the suburbs on the east side of the Willamette had begun to grow. In the summer of 1892, a shocking crime in the suburbs near Sellwood shook the city, bringing Portland closer to a lynching than it had ever been and signaling a loss of innocence and the beginning of the modern urban age in Portland.

On June 22, 1892, school was out, and Mamie Walsh, fourteen, the daughter of a prominent Milwaukie farmer, was staying with family friends, the Luellings, near the Willamette River just south of Sellwood, which hadn't yet been annexed by Multnomah County. That day, she went out to pick berries by the river at about 4:00 p.m. She didn't come back. Soon, Alfred Luelling enlisted neighbors to search for the missing girl. Shortly after dawn, Mamie's body was found. She had been raped and strangled. Her underwear, hat and bucket were missing. The search party turned into a posse, determined to find and lynch the killer. It wasn't just Clackamas County that went wild looking for the killer. On Friday morning, the day after the body was found, Ernest Richards, a German immigrant, was arrested in Portland on suspicion of being the killer.

The Clackamas County posse was pursuing a vagrant who had been seen in the Milwaukie area for the last few months. He disappeared the night of the murder. The posse traced him to Oregon City and then to Clackamas Heights, where they lost his trail at about 5:00 a.m. on Friday. That afternoon,

The Morrison Bridge opened in 1887, making transportation to the east side easier and stimulating growth in Portland's suburbs. *Photograph by Isaac Davidson. Courtesy of oldoregonphotos.com.*

the Clackamas County sheriff, William W.H. Samson, offered a reward of $375 ($8,900 in 2013) for the suspect. A short time later, Tim Sullivan was arrested wandering in Hillsboro, dead drunk; he had blood in his beard, and he roughly matched the description of the suspect. Marshall Loman of Hillsboro telegraphed to Oregon City claiming that they had the suspect in custody and that he had confessed to the rape and murder.

Sullivan had two wounds on his temple. One was just a scratch, but the other was deep and had bled profusely. Sullivan's clothes were stained with blood. In his pocket, he had a Southern Pacific Rail ticket from Cornelius to Portland dated June 23. Election cards in his pocket indicated that he had been in Portland on Monday. Drunk, he claimed that he had been in Milwaukie on Wednesday and said that he had "done up that Luelling family." Under interrogation, he confessed to raping and killing Mamie Walsh. He said that after killing the girl, he crossed the river and walked half a mile on Farmington Road, where he discarded Mamie's bucket and hat. He didn't know what had become of her underwear.

The next day, Sullivan, now sober, proved that he was a homeless man who had spent most of the last year in the Multnomah County jail. He could prove his whereabouts for the last week, and he had not been in Milwaukie on Wednesday. It was clear that Sullivan was not the killer. As the best suspect, he was held without charges in the Clackamas County jail, which was surrounded by a large crowd of citizens ready to take justice into its own hands.

"Work of a Fiend"
Oregonian, June 24, 1892

Irate citizens remained around the Clackamas County Courthouse for days, intent on lynching Mamie Walsh's killer, but now there were too many suspects from which to choose. Multnomah County was holding Ernest Rafes (aka Richards), a German immigrant and organizer with the radical People's Party/Farmer's Alliance. He had retreated to the wilderness along the Willamette River to write political tracts and prepare for the upcoming presidential election. Unluckily, he had been living in a hut he built from tree bark about 125 yards from where Mamie Walsh's body had been found.

Late on Thursday, June 23, A.A. Demules, thirty-five, a piano tuner well known in Milwaukie, was arrested in Sellwood for exposing himself to two little girls about an hour after Mamie Walsh was killed. He admitted that he was in Milwaukie on Wednesday and that he was returning to Sellwood at about the time of the killing. Dr. J.W. Powell examined Demules and declared that he could not be the killer, implying that the man was incapable of committing rape.

Dr. Powell's examination of the young woman's body revealed some interesting evidence. Powell concluded that her body had been washed after the killing. He found a large bruise and some scratches on her thighs and an impression on her abdomen that looked like a key. Crush marks on her forehead were believed to have been made by a boot heel, illuminating the brutality of the killing.

Oregon did not follow scientific detection procedures in the 1890s. Police tended to arrest suspects and hold them for days without charges. They used the hostile crowds surrounding the Clackamas County jail in Oregon City to pressure suspects into confessions. Hordes of sightseers trampled the area around the crime scene. Some of the best investigation was conducted by amateurs, such as Dr. J.H. Hickman, who took a great interest in the case and spent several days tramping the woods along the river looking for clues.

Mamie's body had been placed deep in the woods behind a fallen tree and partly covered with broken branches. Her killer had taken great pains to hide the body, but in his haste, he had left some clues. For one, the collar of her dress had caught on some branches and ripped loose from the dress. The hanging collar had led searchers to the hidden body. A broken barbed wire fence seemed to explain the scratches on the girl's thigh, and a piece of her stocking was found stuck on one of the barbs. Police believed that the girl had been killed, washed and then carried to the woods, where she was hidden. An *Oregonian* reporter retraced the girl's path through the woods and explained that the spot where she was probably killed would have been visible to someone working in the yard of Frank Wilson, the Luellings' nearest neighbor.

Police found that the Wilson family was away from home on the day of the murder, except for Frank's brother from Iowa, Charles. Charles Wilson had come to his brother's farm to work around the beginning of June. On the day of Mamie Walsh's death, he had been working on the fence near where the girl was killed. Wilson said that he had seen Mamie on the day of her death. She was picking berries. He said that he saw three Chinese men also picking berries near where the girl was. He said that shortly after seeing the girl, he had gone back to his house for a drink of water. When he returned, the girl and the Chinese men were gone.

Police did not believe Wilson's story, and some said that he was the first and the best suspect, but he was not arrested right away. Wilson was an English speaker related to a prominent landowner. The suspects who were being held without charges were recent immigrants and/or transients.

On Saturday, June 25, Dr. Hickman discovered Mamie's bucket. It had been crushed by someone's foot and hidden under a pile of tree bark near the front door of Ernest Rafes's lean-to. Submerged in a nearby hollow tree stump made into a water cistern, the doctor found a hook that Mamie had used to carry the bucket. The doctor theorized that Mamie's body may have been washed in the cistern as well. Hickman now became a part of the official investigation, as he confronted Rafes in his jail cell with the evidence found at his place. Rafes was unconcerned about the evidence. He asked why an intelligent person would hide evidence of a murder he committed so near his campsite. He said that he had never seen the girl and was innocent of any crime.

Rafes was a radical vegetarian and pacifist. He found his incarceration, especially for such a violent crime, a very painful experience. Rafes, whose native language was German, passed a note to an *Oregonian* reporter from

In 1891, East Portland and Albina, separate cities, were annexed into Portland, more than tripling the city's population and land area. *Photograph by Cheney. Courtesy of oldoregonphotos.com.*

his prison cell. In this note, Rafes said (with idiosyncratic spelling), "I have a strong hope in truth, justes and rightousness. If I did rong by camping and trying to be alone one week I am willing to suffer for the amount of injustice I thar by did to god and men. Please let me be free as soon as possible. Consider yourself in my place." Things looked bad for Rafes, but many pointed out that he had been in custody since the time of the killing and had not been at his lean-to. Anyone could have come there and planted evidence against him.

Tim Sullivan was soon released. Demules was also cleared of the killing but was held to face charges of indecent exposure. There was a strong circumstantial case against Ernest Rafes, and he remained in custody, but most believed that the killer was still on the loose.

Charles Wilson was the one most people suspected, but his connection to the landowning Wilson family kept the police from arresting him without charges, as they did with the transient suspects. Wilson was not only the last person to see Mamie Walsh alive, but his story of what happened that day kept changing. First he claimed to see the sinister group of Chinese men, and then he said he saw a mysterious man with a satchel near where the police thought Walsh had been killed. After the girl's bucket had been found near Rafes's lean-to, Wilson claimed to have seen the man the day before the killing crawling through the bushes with a guilty "hangdog" expression on his face. When police asked Wilson how this strange behavior before the killing reflected on Rafes's guilt, Wilson said that it was self-evident but did not elaborate. Wilson's strange tales only made him look guiltier.

Dr. Hickman, who was now an official investigator, believed that the evidence had been planted at Rafes's lean-to to implicate him in the murder. He believed that Wilson was the killer but was frustrated that the police still refused to arrest him. He and the sheriff's deputies, along with Mamie's father and her brother, continued to search the weed-covered ground near the river looking for anything that could shed light on the killing.

On Thursday, June 30, searchers found a hammer in the weeds not far from where Wilson had been working, less than sixty feet from the spot where the girl had been killed. Upon examination, the shape of the hammer matched the crush marks found on the girl's forehead. At first, doctors had assumed that the marks had been left by the heel of a boot, but now they knew that they had been left by Charles Wilson's hammer. The evidence was finally enough to arrest Wilson. He was arrested that same day at the waterworks in Riverside. Since Riverside was in Multnomah County, whose county line would soon be extended to cover Sellwood, Wilson was held overnight in Portland.

On Friday, Portland police chief Joseph Purdom went to Milwaukie with two deputies. They met up with Mike Walsh, Mamie's father, and her brother, Richard. Richard and Mike went along with Purdom as they retraced the girl's steps on the last day of her life. When they reached the site near the river where the girl had been killed, they met two Clackamas County detectives. The six men began an intensive search, looking for the missing button from Mamie's underwear. The feeling was that if they could find the button, proving that the girl had been killed where they believed she was, they would have enough evidence to convict Wilson. After three hours of searching, Mike Walsh found the small pearl button less than thirty feet from where the hammer was found. That afternoon, Wilson was moved to Oregon City. At about 3:00 p.m., crowds began to gather around the courthouse calling, "Get a rope! Lynch him!"

Wilson was nearly in panic as he was moved from the steamer that had brought him from Portland. He begged his jailers, "Please don't let them hurt me." His whole body trembled with fear, and he was hardly able to talk. Once in the jail, still trembling with fear, Wilson proclaimed his innocence. He said that if the mob did anything to him, he should be buried in the same cemetery as Mamie because he was as innocent as she was.

Confronted with the button found near where he had been working, Wilson said, "So help me God, I am innocent." Upon being returned to his cell, jailers heard glass breaking and searched Wilson. They found a piece of broken glass in Wilson's pocket and thought that he planned to kill himself with it. During the search of his clothes, guards found that he had a key tied to his suspender. This seemed to explain the impression of a key found on the girl's abdomen.

Wilson was subjected to "stiff" interrogation but still refused to confess. The third degree lasted for hours at a time, and he was interrogated several times that evening. At about 1:00 a.m., police allowed the prisoner to be visited by a clergyman. Wilson, who had been making proclamations of his innocence and his faith in God, spoke with the minister, Reverend E. Githens, for about an hour.

An intrepid *Oregonian* reporter, who had a few exclusive interviews with the prisoner, sent a dramatic dispatch early that morning. He reported that Wilson was in fear that the people in the mob outside would torture him horribly before they killed him. He vowed to kill himself before he would let them get their hands on him. The dispatch ended with this line: "It is at this writing 3 A.M., almost certain that all danger for the night has passed." Shortly after 3:00 a.m., Wilson began to knock on the door of his cell. When a guard appeared, he said that he was ready to talk. He said that he would talk to his brother, Frank, and to Sheriff Samson. He was finally ready to tell what happened to Mamie Walsh.

Wilson talked for hours to his brother and the sheriff. Later, he summed it up for the *Oregonian* reporter:

> *I was working that Wednesday afternoon, digging post holes a short distance from my brother's house. I saw Mamie picking berries and when she approached within a short distance of me, an uncontrollable desire to kill her overcame me. I thought how easily I could kill her. Like a hound after a rabbit, I sprang at her. It took me just three bounds. I grasped her by the throat before she knew my intention. She was a pretty little thing and so innocent. She struggled hard, but could make no outcry, for I had a firm hold on her throat.*

Wilson described strangling and beating her to unconsciousness. Thinking she was dead, Wilson said that he "mutilated her somewhat." He then "examined" her body and realized that she was still breathing. He put his hand over her mouth and smothered her to death. He went on to explain

In 1892, Sellwood was a rural area that was very distant from Portland. As electric streetcars developed, Sellwood became an important transfer point on the car lines, swallowing up large patches of farmland. Mamie Walsh was killed in a strawberry patch not far from where this photo was taken, although the railroad tracks weren't there yet. *Courtesy of SMILE.*

how he carried her body into the woods and left her behind the stumps. He explained that one injury to the girl's head had occurred when he dropped her corpse. He also described how her leg had been scratched on the barbed wire fence. Having "never had any experience at carrying bodies," he was nearly exhausted by the time he hid the girl. He said that her hat and bucket were left in plain sight along the trail he had taken into the woods. He was very surprised that the searchers had not found them. He was worried that people suspected him of the girl's death, and when he heard about Rafes's arrest, he moved the bucket to throw more suspicion on Rafes. He tried to burn her hat, but it was wet, so he buried it along the trail.

There were two glaring omissions in Wilson's story of the crime. First, he did not tell of washing the body after Mamie was killed. No one ever seemed to have noticed this omission. The second was noticed, though. Wilson not only did not confess to rape, he denied it vehemently. After Wilson finished his story, the *Oregonian* reporter questioned him on this issue.

"Did you not outrage the girl?"

"No, I did not. I have told everything and expect to be hung for the crime."

"But the physicians say that an examination shows that she was outraged."

"Then I did not do it and it could not have been done."

"What possessed you to kill her?"

"I can't tell. When I saw her there I became like a wild beast and I leapt upon my prey."

"Now confess to me, was not your purpose in seizing her to outrage her?"

"Yes (after some hesitation) it was. That was my purpose in going after her. But after I had choked her and dragged her into the bushes, my desire had left and I only thought of the dead body. Yet I did not touch her. I think you should believe me in this respect, after all I have told."

Later that morning, the *Oregonian* reporter, accompanied by Mike Walsh and Frank Wilson, searched the area where Wilson said he buried Mamie's hat. After a long search, they found the hat buried about six inches underground. Mike Walsh immediately recognized it as the hat his daughter wore.

The mob around the Clackamas County jail, which numbered more than three hundred, now changed its plans. The people were no longer calling for a rope. The plan now was to burn Charles Wilson alive. Sheriff Samson knew that he would not be able to protect Wilson from a determined mob. After consultations with Multnomah County sheriff Penumbra Kelly and Portland detective Joe Day, Samson decided to move the suspect to the Multnomah County jail in Portland.

Wilson was moved to Portland at about 2:00 p.m. By 5:00 p.m., the crowd around the Multnomah County jail numbered about four thousand. An organization was formed under W.H. Hooper, a Milwaukie farmer and neighbor of Frank Wilson, for the purpose of rushing the jail and seizing Wilson. Sheriff Kelly stood at the front door and demanded that the mob disperse. Hooper and his men persisted in their assault on the jail until they were finally arrested at gunpoint. Kelly then announced that Wilson was not in the jail and was being held elsewhere.

When the crowd still failed to disperse, Kelly took the unprecedented step of allowing an elected delegation to inspect the jail to see that Wilson was not there. Three separate inspection committees were elected, inspected the jail and then were denounced by the crowd. By 1:00 a.m., the crowd had dwindled to about 150, and Sheriff Kelly felt that the danger had passed. Wilson secretly spent the night in the Albina jail.

The next day, Governor Sylvester Pennoyer agreed to hold Wilson in the Oregon State Penitentiary in Salem until he could be tried for Mamie Walsh's murder. That afternoon, with forty burly, armed Portland policemen inside the building, fifty specially deputized "Deputy Sheriffs" patrolling the streets outside and a noisy crowd of about three hundred hurling abuse, Sheriff Kelly and Deputy Billy Morgan took Wilson to the train station. While waiting for their connection at the McMinnville Station, Wilson was recognized, and a crowd began to form. Kelly and Morgan obtained a closed carriage and continued on to Salem. Kelly drove, and Morgan sat inside with the prisoner.

Wilson showed no remorse for the crimes he said he committed, but he did show extreme fear of the crowds that threatened to burn him. He was trembling visibly for most of the trip. The policemen who accompanied him were alternately disgusted by the prisoner and consumed with fear themselves. Passing through the small town of Wheatland, about halfway between McMinnville and Salem, where the infamous Scott murder had taken place in 1890, the men saw a crowd gathering around the local schoolhouse. The crowd was gathering for an unrelated community meeting, but the three men in the carriage were in a state of extreme paranoia. Kelly said that he could see a crowd gathering in the road. At that moment, Wilson yelled, "Look out!" and leaped from the carriage, dashing into the woods. Morgan, tripping over a lap blanket, soon lost the prisoner.

"LYNCHING IN SIGHT"
Oregonian, July 1, 1892

Wilson remained at large for five days, wandering through Dayton. He was finally captured at Chehalem on July 8. While he was loose, the fury of the public became even more intense. A public indignation meeting in Oregon City unanimously passed a resolution saying in part:

Whereas, Sheriff Kelly, suffering even greater cowardice and stupidity than that of Sheriff Samson...permitted said Wilson to escape from him…Resolved…that Sheriffs Samson and Kelly are absolutely unfit and unqualified in courage, discretion and intelligence to hold any position of trust or responsibility, and that both of said sheriffs should be compelled… to resign the positions they now hold, and retire to the well-earned obscurity of private life.

Sheriff Samson, who was still in Portland, decided that it was not safe to go back to Clackamas County, so he joined Sheriff Kelly and the search parties near McMinnville.

On July 8, Charles Wilson was captured near Chehalem by John T. Carter, the newly elected constable of Chehalem and Newberg. By the time he was captured, Wilson was ragged and hungry. He fought back with a razor, but Carter broke Wilson's arm with a club. The beaten fugitive said, "Well, boys, I give up. I am the man who killed the girl and I wish you would kill me at the jail here." He was transported to the state prison right away.

Wilson seems to have lost touch with reality somewhere along the way because after his capture, he began to alternate between boasting over his crimes and begging for the chance to kill himself. Twice he tried to hang himself in his cell, and once he beat his head against the door so severely that it damaged the frontal part of his brain—at least that's what the guards said. Doctors who performed Wilson's autopsy at first thought that he had brain damage that made him kill, but someone pointed out that the damage was probably caused by the suicide attempt. Wilson became known as a biter. During the scuffle with Constable Carter, Wilson bit Carter's little finger very badly. He was also reported to have bitten one of his guards who wasn't paying close enough attention. Finally, Wilson bit his own wrists in another apparent suicide attempt. He bit his wrists so badly that he had to be placed in a straightjacket.

At the state prison, Wilson claimed that he knew "all about" the Scott murder. William Scott, a "gray-haired old man," was serving a life sentence for killing his wife near Wheatland, where Wilson had escaped from custody. Although Scott was convicted, he denied the crime, saying that he had seen a man run into the woods after hearing the shot that killed his wife. Wilson said that in a few days, he would tell what he knew and clear Scott.

Wilson did not ultimately confess to the Scott murder, and since he had been in Iowa at the time of the Scott killing (February 1890), his confession would have been worthless. He confessed to several more killings, some in Iowa and one of a contortionist in a traveling carnival in which Wilson had performed as an acrobat (under the name of Will Rennie). Investigation with

Charles Wilson's ghost was said to haunt his cell in the Old Clackamas County Courthouse for years after his suicide there. *Courtesy of oldoregonphotos.com.*

Iowa authorities showed that there were no unsolved crimes to correspond with Wilson's stories. His family had a good reputation, and Wilson had been known as a "good boy."

After a week of Wilson's increasingly odd and disruptive behavior, authorities decided that the public had cooled down enough, and Wilson was moved back to the Clackamas County jail. A few days after returning to Oregon City, Wilson finally succeeded in killing himself. He unwrapped the bandages on his broken arm, tied his neck to the bars of his cell and threw his body in such a way that his neck was broken.

It was an unsatisfying end to a troubling case. The public hysteria, inept police work and Wilson's odd confessions cast serious doubt on his guilt. Either he really was the "Milwaukie Monster" and put on a crazy act after getting caught, or he was an innocent man driven insane by horrible circumstances. Maybe he was covering up for someone else. The fact that the body was washed tends to suggest that the killer knew the victim. Charles Wilson did not know her. The fact that he did not mention washing the body in his confession leaves some doubt, but the fact that he knew where the girl's hat was buried tends to support his guilt. Rumors of child molestation clung to another neighbor, Nathan B. Harvey, and he was considered a suspect in Mamie Walsh's death when his connection to another murder, in 1911, came out. Could a jury have done any better in 1892? Maybe not. We can never know.

The cell in the Clackamas County jail in which Wilson died gained the reputation for being haunted. This reputation was enhanced in 1916 when Toni Carboni, an Italian laborer on the Bull Run construction project, hanged himself in the same cell. Carboni was being held for killing a co-worker in a knife fight. The building was finally destroyed in 1935.

Hysteria did not end with Charles Wilson's death. Penumbra Kelly faced charges of corruption unrelated to the Walsh case and was expelled from office. After Wilson's death, Sheriff Samson announced that Wilson would be buried in the Oregon City Cemetery in what was known as the "suicide's corner." Somehow, Wilson's body was buried instead in the main part of the cemetery, between the family plots of two prominent families, the LaTourettes and the Nobles, and near the grave of Dr. McLaughlin, the Hudson Bay trader who founded Oregon City and was one of the most cherished figures of Oregon history. The LaTourettes and the Nobles sued to have Wilson's body disinterred and reburied away from their family graves.

Beneath the Mountain of Gold, 1893

Chinese immigrants began coming to Portland as soon as the city was established. The Tong Sung Restaurant and Boardinghouse opened in Portland in 1851, providing Chinese food and housing for contract laborers who worked in a variety of industries. Immigration was slow; by 1860, there were twenty-eight Chinese in Portland, including four women. Most of the Chinese immigrants were young men from Kwangtun Province who saw America as the "Mountain of Gold," a place where they could acquire riches through hard work and return to their homeland as powerful men. Some men, usually those who had capital to begin with, did acquire riches and become powerful on both sides of the Pacific. Most of the Chinese immigrants, on the other hand, owed huge debts to the organizations that provided their travel across the ocean—debts that they could never earn enough money to pay.

In 1852, the first laws were passed that barred Chinese people from owning property in Oregon, and in 1882, Chinese immigration itself was made illegal. In addition to legal discrimination, Chinese faced hazing and harassment from individuals that often became harmful and even fatal. More than one immigrant drowned in the Willamette because some logger or farmer thought it would be fun to throw him off the ferry to see if he could swim. As the Chinese population grew, Portland's Chinatown developed between Taylor and Pine Streets and from Third Street down to the river. The heart of Chinatown was near the corner of Second and Oak Street, where the Joss House and the Chinese Theater were located. Coincidentally, that was where the police station was located as well.

In the 1880s, the Knights of Labor and other labor organizations built their strength by vociferous opposition to Chinese workers. In 1885 and 1886, mobs expelled Chinese workers from most of the cities in the Pacific Northwest, with the exception of Portland. Refugees from Seattle and smaller towns gathered in Portland, increasing the population of Chinatown and creating a situation of very dense crowding. While the Chinese did not face expulsion from Portland, official and unofficial harassment increased.

Because of the intense discrimination the Chinese faced, they were excluded from most services in the city. So, as many immigrants did, they depended on fraternal and benevolent associations to help protect them and provide the services they needed. Tongs, or secret societies based on Chinese cultural institutions, developed to serve this purpose, protecting their members and providing for their needs in various ways. Young men, far from home with hard jobs and low pay, needed diversion from their virtually enslaved condition. The tongs provided this diversion in various ways.

Gambling, a traditional Chinese social activity, was a popular diversion, and it also provided a lucrative business for the tongs. The City of Portland was ambivalent about gambling, sometimes enforcing laws against it but most of the time ignoring it. Opium use was another diversion provided by the tongs. Opium smoking had been introduced to China in the 1850s by British colonialists during the Opium Wars, and it became very popular among the working class. Legal in the United States before 1908, opium became a popular diversion for both Chinese and non-Chinese in Portland. Laws against prostitution were selectively enforced during the nineteenth century, and some of the tongs imported women as indentured prostitutes. These lucrative businesses created great wealth for the tongs, but they also provided grounds for violent rivalries among the societies. Involvement in illegal and semi-legal activities encouraged the development of criminal organizations within the tongs.

Most of the tongs were never involved with illegal activity and functioned much as the Moose and Elk Lodges functioned for Portlanders with European ancestry. Chinese cultural values and strong family and regional ties among the members made them fiercer in defense of their members than Moose or Elk ever became, though. Membership in one of the societies, even one opposed to violence, meant a commitment to defend fellow members and avenge their grievances, even to the point of war. Some of the criminal tongs became highly organized and functioned more like the Italian families who were forming for similar reasons in New York and other East Coast cities. Conflicts often developed between these

By 1900, more than half of Portland's population had migrated from other countries. More than one quarter of Portland's foreign born were Chinese—the city's largest national group. *Photograph by Arthur McAlpin. Courtesy of oldoregonphotos.com.*

more criminally minded tongs, and from time to time, there was open warfare over lucrative gambling, prostitution and opium trades.

In order to enforce their will, criminal tongs began to hire young gunmen, known as highbinders. A few highbinders lived in Portland, but most of them were located in San Francisco and traveled to any community where violence threatened or was needed. The highbinders enforced the will of their employers mercilessly and often in public. Intense public violence created an atmosphere of terror that helped keep the working class under control. One of the most blatant public acts of violence occurred in Portland's Chinatown on December 2, 1888, in front of Frank Woon's restaurant on Second Avenue near the corner of Alder.

Woon was a founding member of the Hop Sing Society, a newly formed tong heavily involved with criminal activity. Hop Sing was formed in opposition to the more conservative older tongs that had dominated Chinatown. In order to demonstrate its strength, the Hop Sing Society took advantage of a low-level conflict over a gambling debt with one of the older societies in Portland, the Bowlung Society. On the afternoon of December 2, six heavily armed highbinders stepped out of Frank Woon's restaurant and confronted Mah Bin and several other Bowlung Society members on the crowded sidewalk.

The Bowlung Society members, some of whom were also armed, fought back, and more than fifty shots were fired. Several people were injured with knives and iron bars in the ten-minute battle that ensued. Frank Woon, the Hop Sing leader, was seen by several people standing on the veranda above his restaurant firing into the crowd below with a rifle. At least three people died from the battle, and at least six more were wounded. It was typical at the time for people who had been wounded in street fighting in Chinatown to hide or even skip town, so it is difficult to say how many people were injured and killed. Mah Bin, Ah Sue and Lup Yick, all members of the Bowlung Society, died from their wounds within a few days.

"CHINESE ARE AT WAR: HIGHBINDER TRAGEDY YESTERDAY"
Oregonian, August 14, 1892

Several people, including Frank Woon, were arrested for murder based on eyewitness testimony, but Multnomah County juries were reluctant to accept the testimony of Chinese in court. Some of the discrimination in court was based on overt racism; a few years later, one of the jurors in a civil case involving a Chinese merchant named Moy Lung was quoted as saying, "I will stay here and rot before I bring a verdict for a pigtail." In addition to the prevalent racist attitude, discrimination was based on experience. Before 1888, at least three Chinese men had been executed for murder based on testimony of Chinese witnesses. In each case, there was evidence that the convicted was innocent of the charges brought against him and that he had been a victim of a conspiracy among the Chinese. This experience made some jurors reluctant to accept the testimony of Chinese witnesses.

As a result, none of the suspects was indicted for murder, and no one was ever brought to justice for the three known killings. The Bowlung Society was badly damaged, weakening the position of the Six Societies, the older, conservative tongs. The Hop Sing Society had announced its presence in Portland with authority and began to consolidate power that lasted for more than a century. As late as 1992, arrests of drug dealers in Portland revealed that the Hop Sing Society controlled a good part of the city's drug trade.

Before the twentieth century, murder was not a common occurrence among Portland's Chinese community. As in any other part of the population, occasionally emotion or greed would get the better of someone, and they would kill. With the influence of the tongs, even a murder for personal reasons had the potential to escalate to warfare when society lines were crossed and the urge for vengeance was aroused. After the shooting in 1888, any time violence broke out in Chinatown, people were fearful of a tong war.

Tension between the older tongs and the aggressive new tongs escalated in the 1890s, coming to a head in Portland in 1892 with the murder of Chin Bow Chong. Chong, a prominent young merchant, was a member of the Suey Sing Tong, a newer

Dong Foot You was convicted of second-degree murder in a compromise. It was doubtful whether he fired the shots that killed Chin Bow Chong. The fact that his queue had been cut off meant that he could not return to China. *Courtesy of Oregon State Archive, Inmate Record #3035.*

tong that was loosely allied with the Hop Sing Society. Conflict with the Sam Yip Society (a tong that had been one of the original Six Societies formed in San Francisco in 1850) over lottery games created the immediate conflict. At that time, the Sam Yip Society controlled most of the gambling and tailoring in Chinatown through its member King Tai. Tai operated a prominent saloon, the Temperance Saloon, located three doors down from the Central Police Station at Second and Oak. The Temperance Saloon featured lottery and fan-tan games, both highly popular in Chinatown.

The Suey Sing Tong was a prosperous group that was well connected with Joseph Simon's faction of the Republican Party. The Sam Yip Society claimed that the rival tong was forging lottery tickets in an attempt to take control of the lucrative business, and it refused to pay off on winning tickets. Chin Bow Chong was delegated by the Suey Sing Tong to collect $133 ($3,300 in

2013) on a lottery ticket. Chong went to the Temperance Saloon twice to demand payment and was rebuffed both times. On August 13, he returned with two gunmen. Witness accounts conflicted, but Chong may have grabbed a bag of money and attempted to leave when he was shot in the back.

Police Chief Ernest W. Spencer was sitting in front of the police station when he heard the shots from the saloon just down the block. He rushed to the scene of the shooting and was quickly joined by several officers. Chong was badly wounded but still conscious. Spencer closed the doors of the saloon and arrested everyone on the premises, although no gun was found. A few minutes later, Officer Sam Simmons saw Dong Foot You, brother of King Tai, hurrying down Third Avenue. You was not wearing a hat, which showed that he was in a hurry, but it is unclear whether he was heading toward or away from the Temperance Saloon. Simmons arrested You as a suspect and smuggled him into the jail before he could talk with anyone.

Police Chief E.W. Spencer, who served in office for less than a year because of his zeal in trying to stop gambling, was the first officer on the scene of Chin Bow Chong's murder. *Courtesy of Portland Police Historical Society.*

Chong lived for about six weeks with a bullet in his spine. In broken English, he told an *Oregonian* reporter that he had not seen the man who shot him. Later, a disputed dying statement, allegedly by Chong, identified You as his killer. The Suey Sing Tong hired Joseph Simon to assist the prosecution of the case. The trial was a circus, with witnesses, all employees of King Tai who may not have even been present at the time of the shooting, claiming that You was not there and that another man, Loy Chow, had done the shooting. The prosecution claimed that there was no such person as Loy Chow, but Chong's statement came into question when it was revealed that the interpreter who had written it down was a sworn enemy of Foot You. The street battle of 1888 hung over the proceedings, and every effort was made to settle the crime in court. The jury compromised and convicted You of second-degree murder.

Dong Foot You served only five years of a life sentence and then was pardoned in December 1898. He was pardoned with the understanding that he would be deported, but it was common practice for Chinese prisoners to be pardoned with that understanding and then never leave the country. It was rumored that Foot You had gone to Manila, but nothing could be proven either way. Officially, Oregon couldn't tell the difference between Chinese, and the Chinese community took full advantage of that. This was especially true where women were concerned.

Six months after the conviction of Dong Foot You, another murder, of Gong Fa, a twenty-three-year-old Chinese American woman born in San Francisco, illustrated the precarious situation of these women. Gong Fa, a popular and attractive prostitute, was well known in Chinatown and among both police and firefighters who worked in the area. Her murder occurred at about 9:30 p.m. across the street from the police station in the glare of a powerful electric streetlight. She was grabbed from behind as she walked to the building where she lived, and her throat was slashed to the bone with a razor-sharp knife. Her body and the murder weapon were dumped in the gutter.

Within minutes, police officers were on the scene and found several people, Chinese and non-Chinese, gathered around the body. The Chinese, distrustful of the police and fearful of the highbinders that enforced terror in the neighborhood, refused to cooperate with the investigation. The police classified the murder as a "Chinese crime" and didn't bother to interrogate any witnesses.

Gong Fa's status as a Chinese American woman contributed to her death being largely ignored, except for the journalistic sensation that lasted a few days and was soon forgotten. Asian and Asian American women in the 1890s were considered to be little more than property, a fact that was recognized in the Multnomah County courts. In the year before Gong Fa's murder, there had been more than one high-profile case of competing highbinders fighting in court over the "ownership" of attractive young women. The women in these cases were allowed the right to choose their "husband" from the parties involved, but beyond that, they had few rights. At times in the 1890s, the Multnomah County court appeared to be little more than a slave auction with legal trappings.

"ONE MORE MYSTERY ADDED TO CHINATOWN'S ANNALS"

Oregonian, November 16, 1893

Gong Fa, described in the *Oregonian* as "very pretty—for a Chinawoman," was a valuable commodity. Tension between her "husband" and her "discarded lover" at the coroner's jury that followed her death indicates that her "ownership" may have been in dispute at the time of her death. The murder created sensational headlines in the *Oregonian* for a few days, and then the paper reported in its florid 1890s style, "Gong Fa's assassination may be added to the long list of mysterious crimes that blackens the history of Portland's Chinatown."

The Legend of Bunko Kelley, 1894

B unko Kelley always said that he was framed. He complained bitterly all through his trial on a murder charge that Larry Sullivan was the source of his troubles. Bunko never told the truth, and he always preferred to blame others for his crimes and his problems, but he may have come close to the truth when talking about Sullivan. Larry Sullivan, a professional boxer from Astoria, consolidated his hold on the lucrative crimping trade in 1894 and 1895. Coincidentally, his main rivals in the "sailor's boardinghouse" business either died or ended up in jail with long sentences during those years. Bunko Kelley was only one of them, but Kelley went to the Oregon State Penitentiary in 1895 framed for a murder he actually committed.

Joseph Kelley, known as "Bunko," came to Portland in 1879. He arrived at a time when the port of Portland was just coming into its own, making this city the busiest and most prosperous American port north of San Francisco, even though it is more than one hundred miles from the Pacific Ocean. The Columbia River provided a channel from the ocean, and Portland is the farthest point that the deep-sea ships of the time could safely reach on the river. The Snake/Columbia River system provided access to Portland from the mining region of eastern Washington and Idaho. The Willamette provided access to Portland from the agricultural area of the Willamette Valley and the mining areas of southern Oregon, as well as the abundant timber from this region. The plank road, now known as Canyon Road, provided access to the rich agricultural lands of the Tualatin Valley.

The corrupt economics of deep-sea shipping during the age of sail, built on the exploitation of sailors, provided lucrative opportunities for people who were willing to sell the lives of seamen as a commodity. Jim

The need for manpower on sailing ships created severe social and economic problems in Portland. A group of ruthless men known as crimps took advantage of the situation to organize complicated criminal syndicates. *Photograph by Frank Haynes. Courtesy of oldoregonphotos.com.*

Turk, one of Portland's infamous crimps, had already pioneered the sailor's boardinghouse system in Portland and Astoria, and Kelley soon jumped into that field. The system—based on blatant fraud and treating the deep-sea sailors of the day as a valuable commodity to be ruthlessly exploited and systematically fleeced—provided a great opportunity for amassing wealth for the boardinghouse owners. It took a ruthless man to run a sailor's

Although more than one hundred miles from the Pacific Ocean, by the 1890s, shipping on the Columbia and Willamette made Portland the second-largest port on the West Coast, after San Francisco. *Photograph by Jesse Meiser. Courtesy of oldoregonphotos.com.*

boardinghouse, and Jim Turk was one of the most ruthless. Turk was also addicted to violence, being arrested repeatedly for assault—against sailors, policemen, rival crimps and his own family.

Bunko Kelley, although capable of ruthless violence, was less violent than Turk. Kelley made his reputation by being clever and slippery, earning the name Bunko by his ability to con his victims. His reputation was made when he supposedly shanghaied a wooden Indian from the front of a cigar store—the hapless ship captain assumed that the "sailor" was stiff from drink until he reached Astoria and found out that he had been swindled. The story may be apocryphal, but it is similar to other con games that Kelley played in his career, so it is believable, unlike some other stories that grew into Kelley's legend.

By the end of the twentieth century, the real Bunko Kelley had all but disappeared behind the false front of his legend, and he had become a nostalgic symbol of Portland in the good old days. The truth is that Kelley was a ruthless thief and liar who put little value on human life, other than what he could get for it. In 1894, he was convicted of murder, spent thirteen years in the brutal Oregon State Penitentiary and emerged as a would-be prison reformer. Much has been written about Kelley and his life, but very little has been written about the murder he committed.

In - 1894, Portland was undergoing a major change. The original merchants and real estate developers who had founded and developed the city were either dead or dying, and a new generation was ready to take over. The pioneer days of Portland were passing, and the city was getting organized for the leap into the twentieth century that loomed. The crimping business was seeing the same type of generational change as it was organized to come in line with the new powers in the city. Larry Sullivan was the new power in the North End. In the more respectable part of town, the change was framed around a political struggle in the Republican Party between the forces of Joseph Simon, boss of the state political machine, and those of Senator John H. Mitchell, also of Portland and one of the most corrupt senators in U.S. history.

By the end of the twentieth century, the real Bunko Kelley had all but disappeared behind the false front of his legend. Much has been written about the so-called King of the Crimps, but very little has been written about the murder he committed. *Courtesy of Oregon State Archives, Inmate Record #3364.*

Jonathon Bourne, a morally flexible young man who had made Portland his home after being run out of his native New England and had become the powerful political boss of the North End, was the connection between the two sides of the city. Larry Sullivan, realizing that his control over a large group of transient sailors could be translated into political power, worked with Bourne, providing a group of voters who could be counted on to vote for the right candidate, repeatedly. Together, Bourne and Sullivan wielded a great deal of political power, not just in Portland but in the whole state.

The murder of George Sayres in the autumn of 1894, and the subsequent trial of Bunko Kelley and his coconspirator Xenophon N. Steeves, a

Brickmaking was an important industry in Portland at the end of the nineteenth century. Conflict over a bankrupt brick factory led to the death of George Sayres. *Courtesy of oldoregonphotos.com.*

prominent Portland attorney, brought the conflict between the Portland establishment and its challengers to a head and served as a preview of the chicanery that would paralyze the state legislature two years later. It also served the purpose of helping Larry Sullivan strengthen his grip and consolidate his power in the North End.

George Sayres, commonly known as "Uncle George," was a well-known character in Portland. Arriving in 1862, Sayres established himself as a popular saloonkeeper before moving temporarily to Baker City and Idaho in the 1870s. When he returned to Portland, he had enough capital to become not only one of the most prominent saloonkeepers in the city but also a budding capitalist. In 1890, he went into partnership with William O. Allen, a construction contractor who also had ambitions to be a capitalist and a real estate developer. The two men invested in the Southern Portland Brick Company, with Allen providing most of the money and Sayres managing the brickyard. The firm went bankrupt in 1891, beginning a long legal battle between Sayres, his business partner Wong Hing Tong and Allen.

Tong, a Chinese immigrant who came to Portland on the *Haytian Republic*, a notorious smuggling vessel, would have a long career that included just about every illegal business imaginable. Sayres, desperate for money after a string of unsuccessful business ventures, got involved with his partner's illegal opium smuggling business, providing storage space for the drugs on his property near the Willamette River in Fulton Park, a southern Portland suburb. It was through his illegal opium dealings that Sayres first made the acquaintance of Bunko Kelley.

Kelley did a little business in opium smuggling, but he couldn't even be an honest drug dealer; his main interest in opium was selling "bogus" opium, made of clay, to Chinese customers. Early in 1894, Kelley worked with prominent Portland attorney Xenophon N. Steeves to make contacts with witnesses in the North End. Through this connection, he got involved in a conspiracy against George Sayres's life. Steeves denied it, but in 1895, he was convicted of hiring Kelly to "get Sayres out of the way." Kelly, a notorious liar, claimed that the plot was to kidnap Sayres and keep him on a ship in the lower Columbia until the lawsuits arising from the brick factory case could be settled in favor of Steeves's client, William Allen. He later claimed that there had been no plot and that he had nothing at all to do with Sayres—another Bunko Kelley lie.

Whatever the deal was, on the night of September 26, 1894, George Sayres was lured out of his house in Fulton Park to a place on the Willamette River nearby, known as "point of rocks," in what is now Willamette Park. Sayres was desperate to raise $200 (about $5,100 in 2013) so he could continue his suit against Allen. He was getting old and was short of funds, and all of his hopes for his future were on the suit he had against Allen. Kelley had promised to help him raise the $200 through a bogus opium scam. Whether Kelley was trying to kidnap or kill Sayres, he ended up beating the old man with a slungshot, a nautical tool that was a heavy weight on the end of a short rope handle, and dumping his dead body into the river.

Sayres's body wasn't found for a week, and in the meantime, Kelley had a major falling out with Larry Sullivan. The dispute between Kelley and Sullivan probably involved competition between the rival sailor's boardinghouses, as well as politics. Sullivan was a leading fixer for the Republican Party, while Kelley was an enthusiastic Democrat. Kelley, chronically short of money, had a big deal going to provide sailors for a deep-sea sailing ship that he expected to bring in more than $500 ($12,000 in 2013). This windfall was enough to turn his boardinghouse partner, George Powers, against Kelley and into the camp of Sullivan. On October 2, the dispute between Kelley

Kelly spent several months in the Multnomah County jail waiting for his trial, and then being held as a witness against a coconspirator, before finally being transferred to the Oregon State Penitentiary. *Courtesy of the* Oregonian, *Oregonian Historical Archive, Multnomah County Library, Portland, Oregon.*

and Sullivan came to a head in a street brawl. Sullivan, a professional boxer with a fierce reputation, beat Kelley badly, breaking his ribs and shoulder.

A few days later, Sayres's body was found floating in the river. Kelley, Powers and several other usual suspects were arrested right away. Kelley claimed that he had an alibi for the killing because of his fight with Sullivan and his severe injury, but this ignored the fact that Sayres had been killed almost a week before the fight. Soon the police had gathered a great deal of evidence against Kelley, including his bow tie, found at the site of the murder, and testimony from several sailors who had recently moved from Kelley's boardinghouse to that of Sullivan.

Kelley claimed that he had been framed by his rival, Larry Sullivan. There is evidence to conclude that the bow tie had been planted after the fact. The witnesses against Kelley were all under the control of Sullivan, and the trial was a political circus, with Joseph Simon's men, led by ex–district attorney John F. Caples, for the defense and Mitchell's men, led by then-current district attorney Wilson T. Hume, prosecuting. There is a very good chance that Kelley was framed for the crime, but if he was framed, it was for a crime that he actually committed. Kelley, who had been fairly close to Sullivan until the election in 1892, claimed that Sullivan knew too much about his business. He was probably right.

If Bunko Kelley's trial was a political circus, the trial of his coconspirator Xenophon Steeves, was even more so. Steeves, from a prominent Salem family, studied law at Willamette University and served as state librarian before coming to Portland to practice law. Specializing in property claims and criminal defense, Steeves faced charges of unethical conduct several times before being charged with murder. At his first trial, Joseph Simon himself led the defense team, but Steeves was convicted of manslaughter anyway.

As steamships took over shipping in the Pacific Ocean, the days of crimping and the sailors' boardinghouses slowly came to an end. *Courtesy of oldoregonphotos.com.*

Released on bail, Steeves pressed his case, and after receiving a hung jury in his second and third trials, the charges against him were dropped. Steeves's career was ruined—even in Portland, attorneys who get away with murder tend to be unpopular. His name became a synonym for the miscarriage of justice for decades.

No construction contractor in Portland in the nineteenth century could have been successful without good political connections, and William O. Allen was no exception. Although his name was connected with the Sayres murder through his relationship with attorney Steeves, Allen was never officially implicated or questioned. If Steeves actually hired Bunko Kelley to eliminate Sayres as a witness, it was probably at the direction of Allen. After most of the murder trials were completed, the original lawsuit brought by Sayres and Tong against Allen was finally settled against Allen. Allen's suicide a few days later was seen by many as an admission of guilt.

The Black Mackintosh Bandit and the Great Escape, 1899–1902

The sun hadn't been up long on June 9, 1902. Breakfast was over for the prisoners at the Oregon State Penitentiary in Salem. Some prisoners had just been marched from the chapel to the stove foundry, where they worked. F.B. Ferrell, a guard with a reputation for cruelty, was in charge of the detail. Suddenly, two prisoners broke away from the formation, grabbed rifles that had been hidden nearby and shot Ferrell to death. It was the beginning of the bloodiest jailbreak in Oregon up to that time.

Thus was born the legend of Harry Tracy, who would be idolized by a generation of young people as the "Lone Bandit," the "Oregon Badman" or "King of the Western Robbers." In 1947, Stewart Holbrook, Oregon's great lowbrow historian, debunked the myth by telling the more-or-less true story of Tracy's pathetic career. Still, Tracy is remembered as the one true old western outlaw to operate in Portland.

Born Henry Severn in Pittfield, Wisconsin, in 1874, Tracy dropped out of school at a young age. He drifted west to Wyoming, where he hooked up with a gang of cattle rustlers that worked with Butch Cassidy and the Sundance Kid. Tracy preferred the city, though. In 1897, he was arrested for burglary in Salt Lake City. Never one to stay long in jail, Tracy soon escaped.

Tracy ran to Colorado, where he joined the Hole-in-the-Wall Gang. He was back to cattle rustling and highway robbery. In 1898, after the murder of a boy (William Strong) during a robbery, a posse went after the Hole-in-the-Walls. During a brutal gunfight, Valentine Hoy, a member of the posse, was killed. Tracy was arrested along with three other gang members. One of the criminals was lynched. The other three were convicted of murder, one after being extradited to Wyoming. Tracy went to jail in Aspen, Colorado,

By 1899, Portland was a bustling urban center. Crime, one of the dominant urban issues of the twentieth century, was becoming an important problem. *Photograph by Herbert Hale. Courtesy of oldoregonphotos.com.*

but escaped a short time later after nearly killing a guard with a lead pipe. This time, he ran to Portland, where he hooked up with Dave Merrill, the local bad boy of Vancouver.

They committed their first crime together in Portland on January 3, 1899, when they held up the Second Street Trolley near College Street. They got nearly $10 ($266 in 2013) in change and a cheap watch. They robbed several saloons and grocery/butcher stores. In one robbery, they got nearly $100 in booze but under $10 in cash. They actually missed $40 in gold during that robbery because they didn't search deep enough in the bartender's pocket.

By the beginning of February, all of Portland was on the lookout for the "Black Mackintosh Bandit." The home of Dave Merrill's mother, on Southwest Front Street near Market, was under constant watch. On Sunday, February 5, the surveillance paid off. Dave Merrill was arrested after being found hiding in the bottom drawer of his mother's bureau with a gun. After intense questioning, Merrill revealed that Tracy was expected to arrive in Portland on Monday.

That afternoon, Detective Dan Weiner of the Portland police spotted Tracy, wearing his trademark black mackintosh, approaching Mrs. Merrill's house. As Weiner stepped onto the sidewalk, Tracy became suspicious and put his hand on a gun in his pocket. Weiner, without identifying himself,

Harry Tracy ran with the Hole-in-the-Wall Gang before coming to Portland. He became a famous escape artist long before he escaped from the Oregon State Penitentiary in 1902. *Courtesy of Oregon State Archive, Inmate Record #4088.*

Dave Merrill had been arrested several times in Portland and Vancouver, mostly for small-time burglary, before Harry Tracy married his sister and the two men began a career in armed robbery. *Courtesy of Oregon State Archive, Inmate Record #4089.*

asked Tracy to walk up Market Street. When they neared Southwest Fourth, they saw the Southern Pacific passenger train coming up the street.

"I guess I'll take this train," said Tracy, "So long."

"I guess you won't," said the detective, drawing his gun. They exchanged shots, and Tracy jumped onto the train. He jammed his gun into the engineer's ribs and told him to keep going. Weiner yelled for the train to stop, but the shooting had panicked the passengers, and the conductor thought that Weiner was a robber at first. Finally, he figured out that something was wrong and cut the air to the train's hydraulics.

Tracy jumped off the train near Montgomery Street. Unfortunately for him, on that corner was Wey's butcher shop, which he had robbed only days before. Albert Wey, the fourteen-year-old son of the butcher, recognized the redheaded young robber and grabbed his father's shotgun. The shotgun was loaded with birdshot, but it hit Tracy right behind the ear, causing a terrible wound. Tracy crashed through a few yards before finally giving up.

Tracy was sentenced to twenty years. Merrill got thirteen. Tracy was cocky during his trial, complaining that Portland was a cheap town, hardly worth expenses. The Oregon State Penitentiary was not a nice place for cocky people at the turn of the twentieth century. Infractions were routinely punished at the lashing post with up to 150 lashes. The "Oregon Boot," an infamous leg iron, was also used on unruly prisoners. It was no coincidence that Frank B. Ferrell was among the dead guards during Tracy's 1902 breakout. Many thought that Tracy had killed him in revenge. B.F. Tiffany and S.R.T. Jones, both guards, were also killed. Frank Inghram, a life prisoner who saved a guard's life by tripping Tracy during the jailbreak, was shot in the leg. Inghram's leg was later amputated, and he received a pardon.

It was no surprise when Tracy broke out in 1902. He had done it many times before. Besides the Salt Lake City and Aspen, Colorado jails, he tried to break out of the Multnomah County jail during his trial. He stole a pistol but never managed to leave his cell. He and Merrill both escaped from a

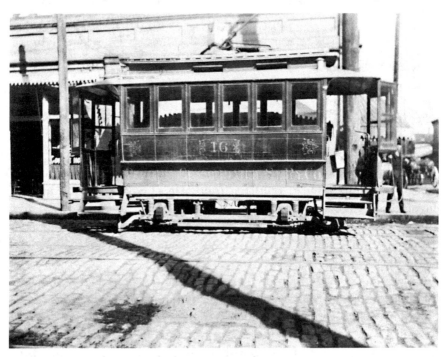

Harry Tracy and Dave Merrill liked to brag about all the money they made from armed robbery, but the truth is that their jobs were small. They robbed streetcars, saloons and grocery stores and never gained more than thirty dollars on a job. *Courtesy of oldoregonphotos.com.*

train platform in Olympia, Washington, in December 1899 after being transported there to face charges. They were both free for New Years 1900 but were captured again in Portland a short time later.

The escape in 1902 was something else, though. Immortalized by a group of pulp fiction writers in the early decades of the twentieth century as a desperate flight for freedom, it is hard to see it as anything else. Trigger-happy posses were formed in every county between Salem and Olympia, Washington, and National Guard units were called out in both states. Bloodhounds were brought down from the Walla Walla prison and put on the trail. Detective Joe Day of the Portland police, who participated in the manhunt, told Stewart Holbrook, "The whole damned country was full of militia, and many of the boys were potted. They shot at everything and Clark and Cowlitz counties sounded like the Spanish American War all over again. It was the most dangerous place I was ever in."

Tracy and Merrill had no trouble avoiding the posses and the rolling batteries of Winchester rifles that dogged them. They moved steadily north, taking food and clothing from anyone they encountered. One time, they even robbed members of the Marion County posse that was pursuing them.

"Where's Tracy? Outlaw Has Completely Vanished"
Oregonian, July 8, 1902

Tracy killed Merrill near the town of Napavine, Washington, on the night of June 28. No one will ever know what really happened between them, but Tracy later told the driver of a boat he had hijacked that it had been a "duel." Evidence showed that Merrill, Tracy's brother-in-law, had been shot in the back. Tracy would be responsible for eleven murders before he was finally run to ground.

A hijacked boat dropped Tracy off near Seattle, sending the gold rush city into a panic. Tracy slipped through the city and crossed the Snoqualmie Pass before shooting himself after being cornered by a small posse near Creston, Washington. He had been free for more than two months when he died.

Before his body could be shipped back to Salem by train, all of his clothes were torn off by souvenir seekers. When his coffin arrived in Salem, it was torn to pieces as well. The more aggressive even tore strips of skin from the body. Tracy was never a successful robber, but he was probably the most successful jailbreaker in Oregon history. Unfortunately for him, that is not a career with a long life expectancy. Harry Tracy was twenty-seven when he died.

The Unwritten Law, 1907

By 1907, life in Portland was changing rapidly; bicycles, automobiles and motion pictures were just some of the new technological marvels that were transforming daily life. In June of that year, a shooting in a boardinghouse on southwest Morrison Street marked the arrival of a new phenomenon in Portland that was sweeping the nation. The "unwritten law" was the Victorian idea that a man had the right to take the law into his own hands if he felt that his family was threatened, by adultery or other means. In the first decade of the twentieth century, there was a rash of murders in which the killers were acquitted by reason of the unwritten law. Each new acquittal seemed to create another cluster of killings, and the trials were highly publicized. In the most famous of the unwritten law trials, that of Harry Thaw for killing Stanford White in New York City, Thaw's attorney called the phenomena *Dementia Americana.*

The shooting of George Hibbens by a former scout of Colonel George Custer, the second case of *Dementia Americana* in Portland, created a sensation and was as highly publicized locally as the Thaw case. It influenced, and was influenced by, other cases throughout the region and across the country. Coincidentally or not, the shooting occurred on the same day, June 19, 1907, that John Bowlsby was acquitted by a Clatsop County jury for a similar shooting that had occurred in Astoria. There would be several more killings justified by the unwritten law in Oregon and around the nation before the first decade of the twentieth century was over.

George Herbert Hibbens, popularly known as Professor Herbert, was a well-known musician in Portland, although he had relocated to Walla Walla, Washington, in 1904. Hibbens had been orchestra leader at Laverne's Outdoor Theater and the Star Theater in Portland before moving to Walla Walla, where

By 1907, Portland had entered the industrial age. Automobiles, electricity and motion pictures were part of the modern way of life. The killing of Professor George Hibbens was a part of the wave of *Dementia Americana* that was sweeping the country. *Courtesy of oldoregonphotos.com.*

he took control of the orchestra at the new Keyler Grand Hotel. Hibbens was married to a popular female drummer from Seattle, but he and his wife had been estranged for at least three years, most likely because of Hibbens's reputation as a womanizer. He was a tall, attractive man with a splendid mustache, and he had the controlling attitude toward women that was common at the time.

Charles H. Reynolds, a former scout with Colonel Custer's cavalry, moved to Portland in 1905 with his two teenage children from his first marriage and his second wife, Lulu, who was more than twenty years younger than her husband. Lulu Garrison, of Salt Lake City, married Charles Reynolds in Pueblo, Colorado, in 1902. Together they moved to Freewater, Oregon, where they ran a hotel, and Lulu pursued her interest in music. Shortly before the family moved to Portland, Mrs. Reynolds's interest in music brought her to the attention of Professor Herbert.

Lulu wrote several verses that she thought would make a good song and took them to Professor Herbert for advice on composing the music. Herbert took an interest in the attractive young songwriter and encouraged her, eventually telling her that if she would give him her love, he would publish her music and make her fortune. The young woman remained faithful to her husband, but Professor Herbert persisted, even after the family had moved to Portland.

In Portland, Charles Reynolds became a partner in a public bathing facility known as the Natatorium Baths. Indoor public swimming pools had become sort of a fad, and every community of any size in the Northwest had one. Portland had more than one, including Reynolds's establishment at Second and Washington. In addition to the Natatorium Baths, Reynolds purchased a large house on Southwest Fourteenth near Morrison that Lulu ran as a boardinghouse. Secretly, Lulu continued to correspond with Professor Herbert; he wrote her daily

Charles Reynolds, a former scout with General Custer's Seventh Cavalry, successfully used the unwritten law to defend himself against murder charges for killing the man he said was having an affair with his wife. *Courtesy of the* Oregonian, *Oregonian Historical Archive, Multnomah County Library, Portland, Oregon.*

letters that he posted to General Delivery, and she replied to him nearly as often.

In 1907, the lives of most women who were deemed respectable were highly controlled in an effort to protect their reputations. Lulu Reynolds spent most her time taking care of the house and the boarders. Charles's two teenage children—John, sixteen, who worked with his father at the Natatorium, and Etta, nineteen, a salesgirl at Meier & Frank—kept a close eye on her and reported her activities to their father. Despite (or because of) the close observation, Lulu took measures to conceal her activities, especially her communications with Professor Herbert. One of her boarders, Miss Rice, acted as an ally and helped with the subterfuge. By that summer, Lulu was planning a divorce, and she and the professor were making plans to run away together to California.

Early in June, Professor Herbert wrote to Lulu Reynolds, telling her that his wife was going to marry Larry Sullivan, ex-boxer, crimp and Portland political-fixer, and that they had run off together to New York. He wasn't telling the truth, as his wife was continuing her career as a popular performer in Seattle. Herbert used the story to convince Lulu that they must take the opportunity to elope together. She agreed to get a divorce from her husband but begged the Professor not to come to Portland. Herbert said that she was his and that he had the right to come, and she reluctantly agreed.

Herbert arrived in Portland on June 14 and took a room at a hotel on Morrison Street, around the corner from the Reynolds's home. In Portland, Herbert bought an engagement ring for Mrs. Reynolds and told her that he would sign over the deed to a five-acre ranch in Ramona, California, to her as a wedding present. The only problem was that she had not yet asked Charles for a divorce.

Charles Reynolds was becoming frantic because he knew that something was wrong, but he did not know about his wife's affair. He was surprised when his wife requested a divorce and immediately began a campaign to woo back her affection. A trip to the Council Crest Amusement Park and offers of dinner out on the town were not enough. Herbert began visiting the Reynolds's home when Charles was at work, staying in Miss Rice's room in order to conceal himself. Sixteen-year-old John Reynolds wasn't fooled, and he told his father that a man was visiting Lulu.

On June 19, Lulu called her husband at the Natatorium and told him that she would not be meeting him for lunch as they planned but that she would be going to the park instead. While they were talking on the phone, Reynolds heard Professor Herbert say to Lulu, "Don't talk to him anymore, Sweetheart." Charles Reynolds went into a rage. He grabbed a handgun and rushed to his house. A few minutes later, Reynolds hurried into his house and found his wife and Professor Herbert in the hallway.

"I'm onto you," Reynolds shouted before pulling his gun and emptying it at Professor Herbert. Reynolds was a good shot, and he hit Herbert several times. Although mortally wounded, Herbert fled the house and didn't stop running until he reached a drugstore a few blocks away. The druggist called for an ambulance, and the dying musician was taken to Good Samaritan Hospital, where he lingered for a few days.

When police arrived at the Reynolds house, Charles Reynolds didn't try to hide. He turned his pistol over to the police and said that he had shot the man because he "despoiled my home." Reynolds proudly pointed to a picture of himself in his cavalry uniform. "Do you see that picture?" he asked. "I was with General Custer for a long time as a scout, and do you think that now, when my home was in danger from a despoiler, I would show the white feather? I will stand by my home."

Lulu Reynolds claimed that she and Professor Herbert were only collaborating on songwriting and nothing else. Reynolds was taken to jail on a charge of attempted murder. Lulu stuck by her story until Herbert died a few days later.

Upon seeing the dead body, she became hysterical and kissed the corpse, giving the lie to her words. Charles Reynolds's lawyers said that they would base the man's defense on the unwritten law.

Trials involving the unwritten law were strangely inverted, with evidence presented against the victim rather than the killer. The defense team was unable to locate Herbert's wife, but much evidence was presented that portrayed Herbert as a cynical womanizer and adulterer. Lulu Reynolds attended the trial heavily veiled and audibly sobbing. She testified for the defense, giving all the details of her affair with Herbert. In addition to the murder victim, the killer's wife also seemed to be on trial.

Although the unwritten law was a major theme of the defense, there was a legal basis for the defense as well. In this case, it was a law that has come to be known as the "Stand Your Ground" law. Section 1757 of Ballinger and Cotton's *Annotated Codes and Statutes* noted:

> *The killing of a human being is also justifiable when committed by any person as follows:*
> 1. *To prevent the commission of a felony upon such person, or upon his husband, wife, parent, child, master, mistress or servant.*
> 2. *To prevent the commission of a felony upon the property of such person, or upon the property in his possession, or upon or in any dwelling house where such person may be.*

Reynolds's defense attorneys claimed that Hibbens's shooting was justified under this law, and Lulu's testimony cinched the case. The all-male jury deliberated for thirty minutes before acquitting the defendant, who was freed that day. Charles Reynolds announced that he loved his wife, although she was disgraced, and vowed to take her back.

"ANOTHER SLAYER ACQUITTED"
Oregonian, October 13, 1907

The unwritten law was an element of male dominance that was often used by abusive husbands or men facing divorce. According to the unwritten law, a husband owned his wife and held the power of life and death over her and anyone he felt was a threat to their relationship. The more the idea was publicized, the more it was used. Just days after Reynolds's acquittal, George Gross of northeast Portland was arrested for making threats against his ex-wife. Gross, who had been divorced from his wife for four years, found her sitting on another man's knee and said, "I should kill you." According to the *Oregonian* of September 24, 1907, "It was a distressing sight and ordinarily would have lead to emotional insanity and the attendant homicide." Since the Grosses were divorced, the husband could only mutter threats and spend the night in jail rather than face a murder charge.

After Charles Reynolds's acquittal, there were at least four more murder cases in Portland in which the killers admitted their crimes but claimed that they were justified by the unwritten law. Most, but not all, killers were acquitted on that basis. In December 1910, George Chamberlain, arrested for stabbing Andrew Massin to death after finding Massin in the bedroom with his wife, was released when the grand jury failed to indict him. Chamberlain was free for Christmas and said that he would divorce his wife, but he complained that without an acquittal he could face charges again at any time.

Not every killer who used the unwritten law defense was successful. In September 1909, R. Thomas Dickerson was convicted of manslaughter for shooting Harry Garrett to death in a case of what Dickerson claimed was the unwritten law. Dickerson and his wife, Martha, had a rocky relationship that had included domestic violence and one divorce and remarriage. In 1909, Martha had decided on a final divorce and was gathering evidence against her husband when he shot Garrett, one of his employees, to death. Dickerson claimed that Garrett and his wife had been carrying on an affair, but she claimed that Garrett was helping her get evidence of Dickerson's infidelity. Dickerson's past abuse of his wife, violent behavior toward others and his own infidelity went into the jury's decision to convict him, but he only served two years before he was pardoned and released.

Women got the right to vote in Oregon in 1912, and this allowed them to be seated on juries. Female jury members did not completely stop the acquittal of killers under the unwritten law, as the last one in Oregon occurred in Curry County in 1919. Nationally, the trend of acquittals under the unwritten law began to abate after the First World War. Although the unwritten law was tried as a defense in Portland as late as 1949 the era of *Dementia Americana* had come to an end.

An Enduring Mystery, 1911

For more than a generation, the brutal axe murders in the sleepy suburban village of Ardenwald frightened Portlanders and brought forth confessions from troubled people. Ardenwald was a bedroom community that had grown during the streetcar boom that hit Sellwood between 1893, when the first streetcar came down Thirteenth Avenue, and 1906, when the Interurban began arriving at Thirteenth Avenue with connections to Portland. Ardenwald, a streetcar stop that was located near the intersection of Johnson Creek Boulevard and Thirty-second Avenue near where the Springwater Trailhead is now, soon developed into a residential area of cheap frame houses on large lots. In spring 1911, William Hill, thirty-two, a plumber who worked for the Portland Natural Gas Company, bought a small house about half a mile up the hill from the streetcar stop. Around May 1, William and his wife, Ruth, along with two children from Ruth's first marriage—Phillip, eight, and Dorothy Rintoul, five—moved in. Here, a short train ride from the city, where William could earn good wages, he and his family could live the rural life that urban Americans idolize so much.

The neighbors didn't have much of a chance to get to know the Hills. The Harvey family, next-door neighbors on one side, remembered Ruth asking where she could buy a cow. The Matthews family, who already had a cow, lived on the other side of the Hills. C.W. Matthews, up early to milk his cow, would usually greet William Hill on his way to the streetcar. On the morning of June 9, 1911, he was concerned when he didn't see William or any sign of activity in the Hill house. He called to his wife that she should check and see if they were ill. Mrs. Matthews couldn't raise anyone by knocking at

Between 1889 and 1913, electric streetcars became an important mode of transportation throughout Portland and spurred the growth of suburbs on the east side. Sellwood's importance grew as the electric trains spread. *Courtesy of SMILE.*

the door, so she peeked into the window. She saw the bloody body of little Dorothy Rintoul laid out on the floor and ran screaming for help.

When the Clackamas County sheriff, Ernest T. Mass, arrived on the scene, he found one of the most gruesome murder sites in Oregon history. Twenty years later, law enforcement officers who worked on the investigation didn't like to talk about what they had seen. William and Ruth's bodies were so entangled that at first the sheriff thought they had only three bodies and that William himself was a suspect. Time of death was estimated at about 12:45 a.m. based on a broken clock in the cabin that was stopped at that time, as well as a neighbor's report that his dog had barked loudly for several minutes starting then. The murder weapon was found to be an axe taken from the yard of R.T. Delk, who had sharpened it and left it leaning against his house, about halfway down the hill from the Hill house.

The family was sleeping when the killer struck. William was dispatched by a blow to the head with the axe handle. He died without waking up. Ruth may have wakened, but she died quickly with two blows from the axe. The children were asleep in an alcove nearby, and it isn't known when they woke up. Phillip was hacked to death, but Dorothy was kept alive and sexually assaulted before finally being murdered. The killer had hung clothes over the windows for privacy, and smeared, bloody fingerprints were found all over the little girl's body. Police believed that Ruth was sexually assaulted after her death as well. Some jewelry was taken, but other jewelry and a purse with cash were left behind, so the sheriff discounted robbery as a motive.

Sheriff Mass, elected to office only weeks before, had little experience and would often turn to outside help in trying to solve the bloody mystery that confronted him. Amateur detectives, psychics and private eyes were involved in the investigation nearly from the start. Sheriff Mass turned to the Multnomah County Sheriff's Department for help, but no police department in Oregon at that time knew anything about forensic evidence

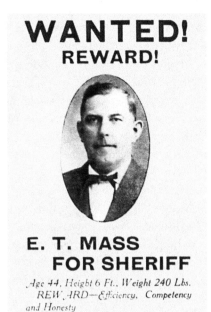

WANTED!
REWARD!

E. T. MASS
FOR SHERIFF

Age 44, Height 6 Ft., Weight 240 Lbs.
REWARD—Efficiency, Competency
and Honesty

Ernest T. Mass was elected sheriff of Clackamas County in 1911. He soon faced one of the most baffling crimes of his career. His handling of the Hill case was one of the main reasons he lost the next election. Four years later, he was reelected and became one of the longest-serving sheriffs in Oregon history. *Courtesy of oldoregonphotos.com.*

or crime scene investigation. Policing in the Northwest in 1911 was more in the paid informant, hidden surveillance and third degree school. Fingerprints, Bertillon method identification of criminals and other scientific methods were looked on with distrust by most police officers.

The nature of the crimes led Mass to believe that sex was the motive, and he pursued that line of investigation. There were a surprising number of pedophile complaints reported in the *Oregonian* at the time. Child molestation is not an invention of the twentieth century, and numerous cases can be found going back into the earliest days of Portland's history. Sometimes the accusations were accompanied by violence, as in the 1892 case of Grant Redmond, who was convicted of sexually assaulting an eleven-year-old girl in southeast Portland. Mrs. A.B. Carleton confronted the man with a horsewhip after her daughter revealed that he had raped her and threatened to kill the girl's family if she told. More often, the young victims were not believed, especially if they were boys, and these crimes were ignored.

Most Portlanders applauded Mrs. Carleton's direct methods; mob violence was always a danger, especially when crimes against children were concerned. The Mamie Walsh murder and the death of Charles Wilson were still fresh in the memories of the residents of the southeast suburbs. Walsh's murder had occurred a few miles west of Ardenwald, coincidently in a strawberry patch owned by the next-door neighbor of the Hill family, Nathan B. Harvey.

Shortly after the murders, there was a pedophile scare at the Arleta School in Mount Scott, a little east of Ardenwald, near the Tremont streetcar stop. One little girl was enticed into the bushes by a gray-haired man while on her way home from school. She ran away and was not harmed. Two other girls reported feeling threatened by a man who made faces at them but did not pursue them. Obviously, some hysteria had taken effect, but the accosting and even raping of schoolgirls has been a somewhat regularly occurring crime in Portland since at least the 1880s. Portland's southeast suburbs have always been magnets for transient oddballs, as can be seen from the assortment of suspects rounded up in 1892 after Mamie Walsh's murder. The Hill case was no exception; in fact, oddballs would continue to confess to the Hill killings for more than a decade.

"Odd Men Held as Murder Suspects"
Oregonian, June 19, 1911

The day of the murder, Ed Ramsey was picked up barefoot after crossing the Willamette on an improvised raft of logs near Oaks Bottom. One volunteer posse spotted Ramsey going into the river and notified police in Portland, who took the man into custody when he reached the west side. After being arrested, Ramsey was found to be the man who had been wandering the east side for the last three years, especially along Johnson Creek, inspiring fear in the residents and minor police complaints. He said that he was a refugee from the 1906 earthquake in San Francisco and suffered blackouts from time to time. He lived in the open, sleeping in the woods, trapping and stealing food. He was soon cleared of any involvement in the Hill murders and disappeared from history.

An unnamed Austrian vagrant who spoke little English was arrested at the Sycamore station on the Estacada line, southeast of Ardenwald, when he took off all of his clothes. He was carrying five sticks of dynamite, a length of fuse and some blasting caps in an old sock, as well as a five-gallon can full of garter snakes. He said that he needed the snakes to "make medicine," but he gave no explanation for the explosives. He had nothing to do with the Hill case, and no one knows what happened to him. U.G. Kightlinger, an elderly man with a record for annoying women, was arrested in downtown Portland, shoplifting lemons, which were in short supply and very expensive. He was considered a suspect in the Hill murders but proved to have nothing to do with them.

Many attempts were made to link the Hill case with other murders, mostly because police were at a complete loss. The murder of Barbara Holzman, whose body was found stuffed under the bed of a Portland rooming house in March 1911, was the first connection. Five-year-old Holzman had been abducted and subjected to hours of sexual abuse and torture before being killed. The sexual nature of the crime involving a child and the lack of suspects led police to see the crimes as linked. A conductor on the Ankeny Streetcar line reported a regular rider on his streetcar as a suspect in both killings. The man was said to be from Tillamook and could often be heard muttering threats to "kill the whole family" while he rode the streetcar. The mysterious muttering man was never found, and eventually someone was convicted for Holzman's murder. Whether they got the killer is still up in the air, but he was definitely cleared of the Hill murders.

"Murderer's Path Traced by Bloodhounds"
Oregonian, June 18, 1911

Sheriff Mass, at his wits' end, tried everything. He had the famous bloodhound Brady brought down from Seattle and put on the killer's trail. Brady, well known to *Oregonian* readers for his work in tracking Harry Tracy in 1902 and several cases after, was given a bloody rag found near the discarded axe. The bloodhound took the scent and led pursuers on a long chase through the woods before losing the trail on a public road. Many believed that Mass had waited too long to bring in the bloodhounds, but the rag had not been found for several days after the killings.

It was with the involvement of two doctors, brothers from Portland, and another bloody murder in Rainier, Washington, that the case seemed to offer its first break. Dr. George A. Cathey was a blood specialist who had invented a spray-on liquid that could reveal traces of blood. His brother, Dr. Collins F. Cathey, had studied the Bertillon method of criminal identification. The two brothers soon convinced Sheriff Mass to let them try their methods. Spraying his liquid at the crime scene, George identified several bloody fingerprints that probably belonged to the killer. Collins measured footprints and fingerprints and soon had a description of the suspect. More importantly, he had made a connection with another case, the murder of Archie Coble and his seventeen-year-old wife, Nettie, in an isolated house near Rainier.

One month after the Hill family was killed, Archie and Nettie Coble were murdered in a strikingly similar way. Attacked in their sleep by someone who broke into the house, Archie was killed with an axe handle; Nettie was raped and then hacked to death. The bloody scene was similar to the mess left at the Hill home, but this time there were no children involved. The Cathey brothers and Sheriff Mass were convinced that sex was the motive in both murders. Collins Cathey compared footprints and handprints at the two scenes and said that the same killer was at work. His brother's formula allowed them to uncover bloodstains in the room of a local hotel belonging to a Swedish railroad section hand named Swann Peterson. Peterson was arrested near Tacoma, and hopes were high that both murders had been solved.

Swann Peterson was a sixty-one-year-old Swedish immigrant working with a railroad gang near Rainier. Bloodstains led George Cathey and the sheriff's posse to room 10 at the Rainier Hotel where Peterson stayed. When Peterson was picked up in Roy, Washington, the next day, bloodstains could be seen on his shirt, although it had been washed. Peterson didn't speak much English, so the police put a Swedish speaker in the cell with him to try and win his trust. According to the *Oregonian*, Peterson told the other man that Archie Coble had been killed first with the axe handle and that the woman had been killed later, by being struck in the head. He also told his cellmate that he had been confined in an insane asylum at one time. When witnesses came forward saying that Peterson arrived in Roy on Wednesday morning and had told several people about the double murder before news had reached the town, it seemed that the noose was closing around his neck.

Swann Peterson may have been the killer of the Cobles, possibly even of the Hill family, but it is hard to judge the methods of the Catheys or the veracity of the *Oregonian* after a century. It is more likely that he had nothing to do with either crime. The case against him had collapsed within a week when another troubled railroad employee came forward. George Wilson was a section foreman for the railroad at Rainier; Peterson had worked for him for six months. Wilson had been among the first to cast suspicion on Peterson.

Wilson had been a troublemaker for a long time, inciting a mob to attempt lynching an accused child molester, John Malqueen, a few months before. It is likely that Wilson had been aroused by the child molestation case because he was a child molester himself. Reporting at the time was coy about the issue, but Wilson was described as a "moral pervert," and the ages of his five children, from one year to eight years, are listed immediately after the reference. Wilson's wife went to the police one week after the killing to say that she suspected her husband of the murders.

When questioned, Wilson immediately confessed to the killing of the Cobles. "There is no doubt in my mind that I killed Archie Coble and his wife," he said, "but I have no memory of going to their home that night." Wilson said that "insane spells" came over him every month, and he would quarrel violently with his wife. About two weeks before the Coble murders, he had been overcome with insanity and fought with his wife. A few days later, while walking in the woods, he heard a voice say, "Why don't you kill someone?" The words stuck with him, and by Sunday, he was afraid that he would kill one of his employees. On Monday, he said he went home after work but slept in a tent because he and his wife were still quarrelling. He woke up on Tuesday morning covered in blood. He could remember nothing of the night before, but he was sure that he had killed someone. When the bodies were discovered, he knew that he was the killer. He confessed to his wife, but she didn't believe him.

"I told about Peterson leaving the camp so that I could convince myself I didn't do it," Wilson said, "But that blood! I'm glad I told about it. I was glad when they arrested me." Wilson soon convinced the police of his guilt but was cleared of the Hill crimes. Despite the testimony of Emily Ferris, a Portland psychic, that her mystic powers told her that he was not guilty, Wilson was charged with two counts of murder. Wilson convinced his fellow prisoners of his guilt as well, though he still said that he could remember nothing about the killings. When two prisoners broke out of the Thurston County jail in November, they carefully locked Wilson up before departing. George Wilson was sentenced to twenty years and sent to the state prison in Walla Walla.

Sheriff Mass returned to Clackamas County, and the Catheys went back to Portland. George Cathey soon moved to Klamath Falls, where he followed his passions for bow hunting, sports and forensic medicine. He was

Sellwood continued to grow, and soon Multnomah County annexed the small city. Now it is an attractive neighborhood of Portland. *Courtesy of SMILE.*

involved as an expert witness in several poisoning murder cases between 1910 and 1925, and in 1946, he was appointed state game supervisor. When he died, he was remembered mostly for his bow hunting, but he was also considered a pioneer in forensic medicine, and his formula for detecting traces of human blood was used for decades. His brother, Collins, continued practicing medicine in Portland and often hunted with his brother. Sheriff Mass continued to investigate a suspect in the Hill murders, but he was keeping his investigation secret this time.

The multiple murders remained a sensation throughout the state. At the end of August, a Roseburg horse thief, calling himself Smith, claimed that he knew who had killed the Hills. Smith, who had been arrested in Marshfield with the horse he stole, was soon exposed as a hoaxer. So, too, were Harry Howard and James Hawkins, two homeless teenage boys who claimed that their companion in robbing a potato field near the Dalles, August Holmberg, had killed the Hill family while they had waited outside in fear for their lives. Howard, seventeen, and Hawkins, sixteen, claimed that Holmberg had kept them as captives and sex slaves. He had forced them to roll drunks and commit petty burglary in Portland during the Rose Festival. On the night of the Hill murders, they said that they had been looking for a house to rob when Holmberg found the axe, but they refused to follow him into the Hill house.

Arrested at the Dalles, Howard, Hawkins and Holmberg were brought to Oregon City, where Sheriff Mass and L.L. Levings, a Portland private detective hired by Clackamas County to assist the investigation, soon broke their story. With a police informer in their cell and the pressure of repeated questioning, it became clear that all the boys knew about the case was what they had read in the paper. Evidence of the sexual captivity of the boys was strong, but they were quickly labeled incorrigible and turned over to the Juvenile Reform School. Holmberg, a transient and petty criminal, was released.

Mass and Levings dug up some interesting information on one of the Hills' neighbors, Nathan B. Harvey. An independent landscaper and forester, Harvey had lived in Sellwood for more than twenty years before moving to a new home in Ardenwald. Harvey was well known in Sellwood and Milwaukie and had a good reputation as an honest businessman. On the other hand, rumor and scandal had followed Harvey for his entire life. When he left Sellwood, there were rumors of sexual molestation of several young girls, but no charges were ever brought. Rumors about the violent deaths that plagued his family were also popular. In 1877, his younger brother, William Corwin Harvey, had drowned while diving off the rocks where Johnson Creek runs into the Willamette. The three Harvey brothers had inherited some money from their father, who died before they left Iowa. Nathan and his brother Daniel invested that inheritance in plots of land in Sellwood and a house in Milwaukie, where Daniel lived with their mother, Mary Bunell. In 1890, shortly after Mary remarried, she was attacked with a kitchen knife while she was sleeping. Her new husband, who had slept through the killing, found her son Daniel dead at the bedside. Apparently, he had killed his mother and then himself.

Mary Bunell and Daniel Harvey were ruled to have died in a murder-suicide, but rumors persisted about the man who had inherited property and more than $10,000 ($237,000 in 2013) in cash from Daniel: his brother Nathan. Rumors increased in the summer of 1892 when fourteen-year-old Mamie Walsh was raped and strangled to death in a strawberry patch near the Willamette owned by Nathan Harvey. The investigation was dropped after the death of Charles Wilson, but the rumors persisted. Rumormongers liked to speculate on Harvey's predilection for young girls and the coincidence of his property ownership. Although the rumors persisted and were publically aired, sometimes in scandalously wrong versions, Harvey had managed to put most of that behind him by 1911 and was at least a somewhat respectable member of the community.

Nathan Harvey spent the day in Portland on Friday, June 9, 1911, the day of the Hill murders. He visited with two other nurserymen in different neighborhoods and then met friends in southeast Portland to watch the Rose Festival Starlight Parade. Then he caught the last streetcar out to Ardenwald, arriving at the station at about 12:30 a.m. Walking up the hill, he passed the Delk home, where the freshly sharpened axe rested against the side of the house, or maybe it was already gone, as he didn't see it. He said he heard no dogs barking and saw no lights in any of his neighbors' cabins, and he arrived home at about 12:45 a.m. He didn't want to wake his family, so he slept in the shed. He slept late the next morning and was startled to find his property overrun by police looking for signs of the murderer.

Harvey, who had been in a property dispute with William Hill since the family had moved in, sweated it out over the weekend, and on Monday morning, he talked his way into the office of Jay Bowerman, a well-respected Portland attorney and former candidate for governor. Harvey told Bowerman that he was afraid that the police would arrest him for the Hill murders, and he begged the attorney to defend him if it happened. Bowerman was not interested in criminal cases and refused, but when Harvey promised him $20,000 ($475,000 in 2013) for the defense and signed over the deed to his home as a guarantee, Bowerman changed his mind. Ten days later, when the police were on the trail of Swann Peterson, Harvey canceled the agreement with Bowerman. When Detective Levings uncovered the fact that Harvey had hired a lawyer to defend him for the Hill case, he shared that information with Sheriff Mass, and they started a serious investigation of Harvey.

On December 21, 1911, Mass and Levings arrested Nathan Harvey, charging him with killing all four members of the Hill family. Harvey had a great many friends who went to work for his defense. The day after his arrest, a story appeared in the *Oregonian* telling Harvey's side, correcting errors in a previous report and quoting statements of support from his wife and his eleven-year-old son. On December 23 and 26, mass meetings were held in Milwaukie and Sellwood, and more than five hundred signatures were gathered on a petition calling for charges to be dropped against Harvey.

Not everyone in Ardenwald agreed with popular sentiment. One Ardenwald homeowner was quoted in the *Oregonian* saying, "Except by his friends, Harvey is feared. There are…those who are possessed of evidence in the case that could incriminate Harvey. If fears of possible retribution from the man are allayed I think they can be induced to tell what they know." Whether the stilted language came from the "man in the street" or the imagination of a reporter, we'll never know. Sheriff Mass and Detective

Levings were convinced that they had the killer, but charges were dropped against Harvey on December 27. Mass insisted that the case go to the grand jury, which it did in January 1912. District Attorney Tongue later admitted that during the secret proceedings, he had ridiculed evidence against Harvey and directed the decision of the jurors in Harvey's favor. No indictment was returned, and Harvey disappeared from history, if not from the rumors of his neighbors.

"CHARGES AGAINST HARVEY DISMISSED"
Oregonian, December 27, 1911

Mass continued to agitate for charges against Harvey, calling for a special prosecutor to investigate the case until Clackamas County judge Beattie put an end to any investigations into Harvey in February 1912. Mass, overwhelmed by the violent crimes that were becoming common in Clackamas County, was ousted at the next election in 1915. In 1925, he redeemed himself and was reelected sheriff, becoming the longest-serving Clackamas County sheriff by the time he retired in 1941. Detective Levings, whose ethics and methods came into question during the Hill investigation, had to sue the county to get the pay it owed him. In 1915, he was awarded $2,000 (about $43,000 in 2013), which was enough for him to retire to an "onion ranch" near the river in Clatskanie. He also donated his extensive files of clippings on criminal cases to the Multnomah County District Attorney's office and endowed the salary of his faithful secretary, Verna Smith, to keep them organized.

Soon the Hill family murders passed into legend, revived by the confessions of lunatics from time to time. Olaf B. Anderson in 1914, Otto Straub in 1915, William Riggin in 1919 and Leroy Robinson in 1931 all confessed to killing the Hill family. In addition, Robinson confessed to a multiple murder that occurred in Iowa on June 9, 1912, exactly one year after the Hill killings. The shocking similarities between the two crimes were probably in the reporter's imagination because no charges were ever brought against anyone but Nathan Harvey.

In March 1916, William Klinkman, an Ardenwald resident who lived within a mile of the Hill home, went berserk at the Ardenwald Elementary School. He threatened to kill the children inside the school and fired several shots, hitting the flagpole. He then barricaded himself in his mother's house

Mental illness, a problem in Oregon since pioneer days, had become an epidemic by the twentieth century. Anyone exhibiting unusual behavior could be judged insane and incarcerated in the Oregon State Insane Asylum. *Photograph by James Crawford. Courtesy of oldoregonphotos.com.*

across the street from the school and held his mother and two sisters hostage for nearly two days before he was finally overpowered by police and taken into custody. The sensation of this crime and subsequent crimes pushed the Hill family murders out of the public mind, and the crime was largely forgotten.

The Dark Strangler, 1926

Forty years before the term "serial killer" was coined, and nearly fifty years before the concept of "sexual sadism" was described, Earle Nelson, known to history as the "Dark Strangler," practiced both. When he was finally executed in 1928, Nelson was charged with twenty-two separate murders and was a strong suspect in eight more. Portland lost four women to America's first sexual serial killer. Portland's Police Bureau, busily trying to keep order in the whorehouses and speakeasies of the North End, was not ready to deal with a highly dangerous psychopath. In fact, it wasn't until Nelson had killed three women and moved on that Portland police even realized that they had all been murdered.

Beata Withers, thirty-five, was depressed about her health and her finances. Divorced for a few years, she had reached the end of her financial resources and was unable to find work because her health had been bad for some time. She faced foreclosure of her mortgage, but her lover, Bob Fretzell, was trying to help her save her house; his finances were slim too, though. On October 19, 1926, she had lunch with Fretzell and her fifteen-year-old son, Charles, a student at Benson High School. After lunch, Beata worked in her flowerbeds, and her next-door neighbor said that she seemed very cheerful. Beata was probably cheerful because she had finally found a renter for the spare room she had been advertising for weeks.

Charles came home after school, but his mother wasn't there. When she wasn't home by dinnertime, he called Fretzell, but he hadn't seen her since lunch. Charles was worried about his mother; he was afraid she might have taken her own life. When she wasn't home in the morning, he called the police and told them of his fears. It took a thorough search of the house

Demand for lumber and wooden ships during the First World War more than doubled Portland's population. The denser population and improved transportation of the 1920s allowed criminals such as the "Dark Strangler" to operate covertly. *Photographer unknown. Courtesy of oldoregonphotos.com.*

before the woman's body was found at the bottom of a trunk full of old clothing in the attic. It appeared that she had smothered to death, and the police called it the strangest suicide they had ever seen.

"POETRY INSPIRES SUICIDE IN TRUNK"
Oregonian, October 21, 1926

The next day, Mrs. M.D. Lewis was doing some work around a small vacant house she had for sale in Sellwood. A beat-up old car pulled up in front of her house, and a small, dark-skinned man got out and walked up the front steps. He was rude and gruff, muttering, "House for sale," as he pushed his way in the front door. Mrs. Lewis took an immediate dislike to the man and his rude behavior. He went up the stairs to look at the attic, but Mrs. Lewis stayed below. After a few minutes, she heard the man's voice from above.

"Come upstairs and see what's wrong with this door," he said. Mrs. Lewis had a bad feeling. Nothing could make her go upstairs with this man.

"The door will be fixed before the sale," she called. A few minutes later, the man stormed down the stairs and went into the basement.

"Come down here and see what's wrong with this furnace," he called. Mrs. Lewis had had enough and she fled the house into the backyard.

"Come and see my pretty flowers," she called.

"To hell with your flowers," the man said and left hurriedly, driving off in his car. A few blocks away, Mabel Fluke, thirty-seven, was holding an open house at the vacant home she had shared with her

Police Chief Leon Jenkins oversaw the Portland Police Bureau as new technology and investigative methods were introduced, but in 1926, the force was not prepared to deal with the highly mobile sexual serial killer known as the "Dark Strangler." *Courtesy of Portland Police Historical Society.*

husband until his death two years before. She had been renting the house since her husband died and living with her parents in St. Johns. Mabel Fluke had spent the day at the house doing minor repairs and meeting prospective tenants, determined to rent the house so she could go visit her brother in Independence without worrying about it. When she didn't come home that night, her parents didn't think anything of it, but the next day they began to worry.

On October 21, Charles Myers and Harold Ries went to a vacant house on Southeast Twenty-second owned by their mother-in-law. Virginia Grant, fifty-nine, who lived in Ladd's Addition, had gone to the house to show it to a renter, but she hadn't come back. Myers and Ries found her collapsed behind the furnace in the basement. They knew that she had heart disease, and they assumed that she had died a natural death. As they carried the dead woman up the stairs to the main floor, one of her diamond earrings fell out of her clothes. The other was nowhere to be found. Two valuable diamond rings that Virginia always wore were missing as well.

That afternoon, Mabel Fluke's father searched the vacant house in Sellwood. No one in Portland or Independence had seen the woman since the twentieth. He didn't go in the attic, but he called the police and filed a missing persons report. It wasn't until October 23 that the police finally searched the attic, which had no lights, and found the body of Mabel Fluke. She had been strangled with a dresser scarf. Some police thought that Fluke's death was another bizarre suicide, but most of them, including Chief Leon Jenkins, realized that she had been murdered. Several questions had arisen about the deaths of Grant and Withers, and Chief Jenkins was starting to think they might all have been murdered.

"3 WOMEN SLAIN BY STRANGLER"
Oregonian, October 24, 1926

Patrolman Russell was the first to suggest that the killings in Portland might be the work of the "Dark Strangler," who had been terrorizing the California coast since February. Russell's cousin, George Russell of Santa Barbara, had written to the Portland policeman in August to tell of the horrible death his wife had suffered at the strangler's hands. Russell thought that the three deaths in Portland were the work of the same killer. Detective Archie Leonard thought that Russell might be right. Most officers didn't agree, but Chief Jenkins thought the idea might have merit. He issued a public warning for women not to show vacant houses alone and asked Mayor Baker for a special appropriation to hire a criminologist and pathology specialist to help with the investigation.

Exhibiting the mobility that would later be identified as part of the serial-killing pattern, Earle Nelson had already returned to San Francisco. He had killed three women in Philadelphia and five women in California, as well as his three Portland victims. He didn't waste much time once he got home. On November 18, he strangled Mrs. William Edmonds of San Francisco, another woman with a room for rent. Nelson was compulsively driving the primitive highway system of the West Coast looking for victims. On November 22, he killed Florence Monks, a wealthy widow with a room to let in Seattle. Monks, a few weeks before, had taken all of her jewelry, more than $10,000 worth ($125,000 in 2013), out of her safe deposit box against the advice of her family. She liked to wear her jewels around the house, and when she wasn't wearing them, she kept them in a fabric bag she had sewed into the inside of her dress.

Nelson usually sexually abused his victims after strangling them and then carefully arranged their clothing as he posed the bodies, to conceal his perversion. He usually took items of clothing or jewelry from his victims, but police believed that these were souvenirs more than for profit. He found Monks's jewelry and took it with him. The jewelry would become the first link in identifying the "Dark Strangler." That night, he drove to Portland, arriving the morning of the next day.

It was Wednesday, the day before Thanksgiving, and things were dreary at the lodging house Sophia Yates ran on Third Avenue south of downtown. Three women in their sixties lived in the house, and one room was vacant. It looked like a disappointing Thanksgiving since none of the women had enough money to buy the fixings for dinner. That morning, a polite young man arrived and paid $2 cash for a week's rent on the vacant room. He said that his name was Adrian Harris, and the women thought he looked like a logger. Better yet, the young man went out and spent $14 ($175 in 2013) on a turkey and all the fixings and asked the women to prepare an old-fashioned Thanksgiving dinner for him.

Harris wasn't feeling well; he had come down with the flu. Yates and one of her lodgers, Emily Cayford, were very motherly toward him. He sat by the fire in Emily's room while she and Sophia cooked dinner the next day. They all had dinner together and were very friendly. The women said that Harris was very intelligent and could speak at length on any religious subject but that he was also a bit of a fanatic. Harris obviously felt affectionate toward the older women, giving both Sophia and Emily several expensive pieces of jewelry he said he had no use for. He gave the jewelry to the women secretly and asked each of them not to tell the other about it.

He stayed five days, looking around the neighborhood for vacant apartments, but neither Emily nor Sophia could keep a secret. Emily found out that Harris had given Sophia more jewelry than he had given to her. That started the women quarreling. They must have gotten loud about it because suddenly Harris burst into the room. "I'm going to beat it," he said. "You two will have the police up next." He ran from the house and drove away, leaving two days' rent unused.

On November 29, 1926, Blanche Myers, forty-eight, had lunch with her teenage son, Lawrence, and Alexander Muir. Muir owned the house that Blanche ran as a boardinghouse in South Portland, not many blocks from Sophia Yates's lodging house, and he had been repairing the roof that morning. Blanche complained about the lack of tenants. She charged more than most of the boardinghouses in the neighborhood because she wanted respectable boarders, but it was having a chilling effect on her business. Her son went back to school, and Muir stayed for coffee and a cigar. While the two friends were talking, a knock came at the door. Muir heard Blanche greet a tenant and take him upstairs, while he stayed in the kitchen. She was gone for about fifteen minutes.

She had a big smile on her face when she returned and slapped seven half dollars down on the table. "That beats a vacant room," she said, and her landlord smiled too.

"What's he do?" asked Muir.

"He looks like a logger," she replied.

"We're a little far uptown for loggers here," Muir said. "Is he a drinker?"

"I asked him," Blanche answered. "He said not much."

"Only when he can get it?" the landlord joked.

Arthur finished his cigar and left Blanche with her new lodger, who was having a nap in his room. She accepted a coal delivery in the afternoon, but when Lawrence returned home from Lincoln High, he found the basement door and the back door open. The "Room for Rent" sign that had been in the window was sitting on the kitchen table. His mother was nowhere to be found. When she wasn't home by midnight, he called the police.

They found her stuffed under the bed in the room that the "logger" had rented. Her mouth was tightly bound by a strip of cloth, and she had put up quite a struggle. Several of her ribs were broken, and blood spatters on the floor had been covered with a throw rug. This time, there was no doubt that the victim had been murdered. It wouldn't be long before everyone knew that the "Dark Strangler" had struck again.

Born Earle Leonard Ferral on May 12, 1897, to a mother in the advanced stages of syphilis, Earle Nelson showed signs of mental illness from an early age. Raised by a Bible-thumping grandmother, Earle showed evidence of sexual abuse at school, and by the age of seven, he had been expelled because of his violent rages. At the age of ten, Nelson suffered a serious head injury. Although the doctor said that he would be all right, this was only the first wrong diagnosis of Nelson's condition.

Earle Nelson was arrested for burglary in 1915 and spent two years in San Quentin Prison. He was released in 1917 at the height of American participation in World War I. Nelson joined the army but deserted after

A diagram of the room that Blanche Myers rented to the mysterious Adrian Harris. Her body was found under the bed. Bloodstains were found under the rug labeled "A." *Courtesy of Portland Police Historical Society.*

six weeks. He began a compulsive pattern of enlisting alternately in the army and the navy, serving a few weeks and then deserting. He did this four times under as many names. In 1918, he was hospitalized by the navy and diagnosed as living in a "constitutional psychotic state." On May 21, 1918, Nelson was described by Dr. J.B. Rogers as "not violent, homicidal or destructive." Wrong diagnosis again.

Nelson escaped from the hospital twice in 1918, managing to stay free for over a month the second time. He earned the nickname "Houdini" from the hospital staff. When he escaped a third time in May 1919, no one bothered to chase him. He was discharged in absentia from the navy, and his mental hospital file was closed with a note saying that Nelson had "improved."

Nelson found work as a hospital janitor and soon married a co-worker who was thirty-six years older than he was. Nelson's jealous rages, bizarre sexual demands and increasingly violent behavior ended the marriage fairly quickly. Nelson drifted from job to job but found his real avocation on May 19, 1921, when he invaded the San Francisco home of Charles Summer and tried to rape Summer's twelve-year-old daughter. The young girl screamed for help, and Nelson was captured. Nelson was confined in mental hospitals, except for a brief escape in 1923, until March 10, 1925, when he was again discharged as "improved." Five months later, he began the killing spree that would carry him to the gallows in Winnipeg, Manitoba, in January 1928.

After the death of Blanche Myers, Portland was in a panic; the city issued new warnings about single women showing vacant apartments. Chief Jenkins sent Detective Leonard to Seattle to coordinate with the police there, and Jenkins went to California to see if he could connect any of the southern murders with the four in Portland. Sophia Yates and Emily Cayford were shocked to think that their polite young boarder might be involved, but they reported the jewelry he had given them to the police. Within twenty-four hours, the Seattle police confirmed that the jewelry the young man had given the two women came from Florence Monks.

The next day in San Francisco, Chief Jenkins tentatively connected the murder of Mrs. William Edmonds in that city to the murders in Portland. Investigators in Portland had discovered a bloody fingerprint in Blanche Myers's room; it was the first physical evidence pointing to the identity of the murderer. Technology was not available to let them search for a match, but photographs of the fingerprint were mailed to police departments all over the country, as well as in Canada. Law enforcement agencies in at least three states began a massive manhunt for the elusive Adrian Harris.

He moved quickly and stayed well ahead of the police. The day before Christmas Eve, he strangled and raped Mrs. John Berard, forty, in Council Bluffs, Iowa. After Christmas, he strangled Bonnie Pace, twenty-three, in Kansas City, Missouri. The next day in the same city he killed Germania Harpin and smothered her eight-month-old baby. By spring, the strangler had reached Philadelphia, where he killed Mary McConnell, sixty. By the end of May, he was in Buffalo, New York, where he strangled Jennie Randolph, thirty-five, before moving on to Detroit. In Detroit, he killed Maureen Oswald and Minnie May. Both women were raped after they died, and Detroit police announced that the murders were committed by the "Pacific Coast Bluebeard."

On June 4, 1927, Nelson killed Mary Sietsma in Chicago before slipping over the border into Canada. Sietsma's murder was his most violent and brutal yet; he was losing control and giving in more and more to

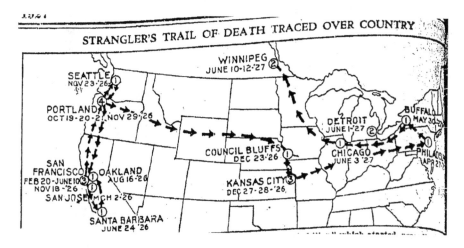

STRANGLER'S TRAIL OF DEATH TRACED OVER COUNTRY

The "Dark Strangler" killed at least twenty-two women as he made his way back and forth across the country. He was finally captured and executed by the Winnipeg Police after a killing spree in that city. The numbers on the map mark the number of victims in each location. *Courtesy of Portland Police Historical Society.*

his necrophiliac urges. Nelson rented a room in Winnipeg, introducing himself as Mr. Woodcots, a religious man. He said that all he wanted was a quiet room where he could read his Bible. Within days, Nelson lured thirteen-year-old Lola Cowan to his room, where he killed and raped her. He stuffed Cowan's body under his bed and left the door open. The landlady cleaned the room the next day but didn't discover the body for three more days.

The next day, Nelson killed Emily Patterson, twenty-three, in nearby Elmwood. He beat her to death with a hammer before raping her. Patterson's murder was so brutal that the Winnipeg newspapers called the killer the "Gorilla Man." A $1,500 ($18,000 in 2013) reward for the killer of Patterson and Cowan paid off with several sightings of Nelson as he made his way toward the U.S. border. He was captured just north of the border early on the morning of June 16, 1927. Murder charges were filed on Nelson in five U.S. cities, including four counts in Portland, but Canadian authorities would not give him up.

Nelson's trial was delayed for several months in order to let public feeling cool off. In November, at his trial, Nelson pleaded insanity, but expert psychiatrists, using X-rays of Nelson's brain, testified that although he was a "constitutional psychopath," he was still responsible for his actions. On January 13, 1928, Nelson was hanged in Winnipeg. On the scaffold before the execution, Nelson said, "I declare my innocence before God and man.

I forgive those who have injured me and I ask pardon from those I have injured." The hangman's rope was a little too short, and it took Nelson nearly fifteen minutes to strangle to death. Some thought it was poetic justice for the "Dark Strangler."

Taken for a Ride, 1933

The year 1933 was a hard one, and not just in Portland. Hitler came to power in Germany, and Franklin Roosevelt almost didn't take office when Chicago mayor Anton Cermak was assassinated right in front of him. The nation had just survived the worst year of what was then known as the Hoover Depression, and all the banks were closed for a series of bank holidays. Money was scarce, and tempers were short; violence flared in labor and farm disputes all over the Midwest and even struck close to home when a mob of unemployed nearly lynched the sheriff trying to evict a family from their home in Seattle. In Chicago, even a public school teachers strike turned violent. The teachers hadn't received any pay for nearly a year.

In the first move to end prohibition, 3.2 percent beer became legal, but there was still a good market for the hard stuff, and bootlegging was a lucrative profession. In fact, it seemed like only criminals had money. Violent armed robbers such as Bonnie Parker and Clyde Barrow, John Dillinger and Charles "Pretty Boy" Floyd gained huge publicity and fed a popular culture that glamorized violence. These public enemies represent the rural criminal response to the Great Depression; in the cities, the criminals organized into semi-corporate entities that controlled areas of vice. These organizations, such as Al Capone's group in Chicago and the New York crime families, gained immense power and capital during the Prohibition era. With an end to the noble experiment at hand, they were looking for growth areas.

In Portland, organized crime has almost always been controlled by locals and heavily defended against outside interests. Crime organizations, other than some of the Chinese tongs, have tended to be fairly small and specialized. Prohibition had created such a great opportunity that bootlegging was the

By 1933, forty thousand Oregonians had registered for unemployment relief, and thousands lived in shantytowns known as "Hoovervilles." Governor Julius Meier wrote to President Hoover, "We must have help from the federal government if we are to avert suffering and possible uprisings." The Ross Island Bridge is visible in the background of this photo. *Photograph by Arthur Rothstein. Courtesy of oldoregonphotos.com.*

one sideline that anyone could have. Frank Kodat kept a speakeasy on Southeast Water Street, near the corner of Yamhill, but his specialty was safecracking. In the jargon of the era, Frank Kodat was a yegg.

On the ground floor was a machine shop that didn't have much work. Kodat's place—a barroom, his apartment and several rooms for rent— was arranged in a sort of a maze on the second floor. Kodat's friend Jake Silverman could be counted on to bring prostitutes in his wife's big maroon Studebaker sedan whenever necessary. The car, which could easily carry six to eight passengers in addition to the driver, was a common sight on Water Street, as well as near Silverman's Riverside Hotel on the west side. Silverman had spent a few years in the state penitentiary for selling stolen Victory Stamps at the end of the First World War, but his main job had always been as a pimp—or as he liked to say, "hotel keeper."

Organized crime in Portland has usually been run by local bosses, who fiercely defended their turf from outsiders. In 1933, Frank Kodat adapted the tradition of sailor's boardinghouses to include ex-cons whom he organized into a burglary ring. *Photograph by Ralph Eddy. Courtesy of oldoregonphotos.com.*

Frank Kodat started his yeggman career as an apprentice to one of the legendary members of his profession, Peter "Dutch Pete" Stroff. Dutch Pete, whom the *Oregonian* called "the hardest man to enter the territory since Harry Tracy," pleaded guilty to train robbery near Portland in 1909 and was sentenced to twelve years in the Oregon State Penitentiary. Stroff had served time in Montana and was known as a gunman and desperado, but his time in Salem was transformative for him. While in prison, he must have studied the fine arts of burglary and safecracking because when he was released in 1920, he began to practice them. Dutch Pete had a genius for organization. He soon had organized a loose network of safecrackers and burglars, based in Portland, who pulled jobs all over the region. Their rule was no jobs in Portland; anywhere else was safe.

Kodat and Dutch Pete got busted for burglarizing the Gold Hill Bank near Medford in 1921 and spent a few years in the penitentiary. They used that time to expand their network and hone their skills. By the time they got out, Kodat took over the organization in Portland and only rarely participated in a job unless it was close to home, like the Gresham job

It seemed like only criminals had money. Portland made a comfortable headquarters for a gang of burglars and armed robbers that carried out jobs throughout the region. *Photograph by Ralph Eddy. Courtesy of oldoregonphotos.com.*

in 1928. Dutch Pete was more of a field man; he never quite refined the stealth necessary for burglary. He seemed to thrive on armed robbery, and he was not slow to pull the trigger. Shootings occurred at many of the jobs in which Dutch Pete participated, including the post office job in Willow Creek, California, in June 1928. An exchange of gunfire killed Deputy Sheriff William Carpenter and John Bishop, one of the robbers. Stroff was caught later that evening near Eureka and soon confessed that he and his accomplices had planned the job together and traveled from Portland to pull it off. Dutch Pete, fifty-two, who had already served twenty-six years in the stir, ended up in federal prison for life.

Frank "Shy Frank" Kodat understood stealth. He publically claimed that he had "gone straight" and that he would work with young convicts to help them get back on their feet so they could go straight too. He went straight to his combination saloon/brothel/rooming house in the industrial east side. The men who rented his rooms were usually fresh out of prison, and they had already been organized, either in prison or before their convictions. Most of them were burglars, specializing in businesses—restaurants and drugstores seemed to be particularly popular. They had given up on the "no Portland jobs" rule by then, and it wasn't uncommon for them to hit businesses on the west side.

Kodat's health was not good; he suffered from tuberculosis and arthritis. He preferred the more sedentary work of planning the crimes and fencing or laundering the proceeds. He was well liked in the neighborhood, and most of the men in his organization were very loyal to him, but not all of them. Jimmy Walker, thirty-eight, was not a loyal member of the gang; worse than that, Kodat thought he had stolen a watch from one of his lodgers. Kodat was a criminal, but he didn't like a thief.

James Walker was a small-time burglar just like most of his fellow lodgers, but he liked to play the big shot. He wanted to be somebody, but he never really was. He must have been a charmer, though, because Frank Kodat's girlfriend, Edith McClain, went for him right away. McClain, thirty-eight, was what was known at the time as a "gun moll." Gun molls were gangsters' girlfriends. She came to Portland from Florence, Oregon, during the war. She was married for a few years, and she had four children, but each of them had been raised by a different family. McClain spent her life among Portland's underworld, drinking in speakeasies and hanging out with criminals, violent and nonviolent.

In February 1933, Jimmy Walker was released from prison in Salem after a sentence for a Klamath Falls burglary. He had served two previous prison terms for business burglaries in Wisconsin and Kansas. When released from the Oregon Penitentiary, Jimmy went straight…to Frank Kodat's place. By April, Kodat and Edith McClain were quarrelling, and she and Jimmy were spending a lot of time together. When Jimmy was accused of stealing a watch, Frank had his excuse to kick him out of his room. The two men fought, and Jimmy took Frank's gun away from him. Frank was upset by the altercation and took to his bed. Somehow, accidentally or on purpose, Jimmy fired Frank's gun in one of the upstairs rooms. The bullet passed through the flimsy wall and hit Frank in the back. Jimmy swore it was an accident, but he knew he was "going to get burned."

Jimmy headed across town to a hotel near the corner of southwest Twelfth and Morrison, where a buddy of his, Ray Moore, was staying. Moore was a drug addict who specialized in "smash and grab" robberies. Jimmy told Moore about the accidental shooting and begged for a ten-dollar loan so he could get out of town. Moore probably gave Jimmy some dope, some form of opiate, and said he would help. Jimmy got word to Edith, and she soon arrived with a small suitcase. She was ready to run because she had all her personal papers and some newspaper clippings about her children's achievements with her meager belongings. She and Jimmy registered as a married couple for a room of their own, and Moore said that he would arrange a ride for them to Astoria.

Frank Kodat was rushed to Good Samaritan Hospital, where doctors decided that his health was too frail to allow them to remove the bullet in his back. Police must have been shocked to find illegal alcohol in his place because they arrested Abe Levine, the well-dressed bartender with a record for robbing clothing stores, as well as William Edwards, a waiter, and Olaf Olsen, the cook. Levine, who had known Kodat since they had been in prison together, was beside himself over the shooting. When Jake Silverman showed up at police headquarters and vouched for Levine, saying that they needed to go find the guy who shot Shy Frank, they released him into the hotelkeeper's custody. According to the unbelievable story the two men told later, Levine spent the rest of the evening in a "malt shop" downtown. Silverman went home, picked up his son-in-law and then dropped his wife's big sedan off at a garage for washing. Both men seem to have forgotten about finding Jimmy Walker.

Meanwhile, Ray Moore got in touch with his old buddy, Larry Johnson, another ex-convict, and introduced him to Walker as the guy who could get him out of town. They just had to wait until it got dark, and a car would come to pick them up. Walker and Edith McClain weren't hard to convince, and they spent the rest of the day in their hotel room, waiting for dark. Ray Moore went down the street to Zell's Jewelry Store on Southwest Morrison Street, smashed the window, grabbed a few trays of watches and jumped into a taxi. It didn't take long for the police to catch up with the junkie, and so he had a perfect alibi for the murder he knew was going to occur.

Larry Johnson got in touch with Jack Crim, an ex-convict friend of Kodat's who was making a reputation for himself as a boxer. Crim was a large, good-looking man—a Modoc Indian from Klamath Falls who claimed to be a nephew of Captain Jack, the chief of the Modocs who led the fierce resistance that killed General Edward Canby near Tule Lake, California, in 1873. Crim, who was not really old enough to have been a nephew of the man who had died sixty years before, liked to take advantage of Captain Jack's fearsome reputation by claiming that he had his "uncle's" war bonnet and ceremonial war club—neither of these items are traditional implements of the Modoc, but few people who admired the boxer knew that or cared. Crim and Johnson went to Kodat's place, where they retrieved his gun.

Shortly before 7:30 p.m. that night, a large maroon sedan pulled up in front of the hotel where Jimmy Walker and Edith McClain were waiting.

Several people described the car. Witnesses said that a man in a wine-colored suit was next to the driver, who resembled Jake Silverman. A large man, answering the description of Jack Crim, helped Edith McClain into the backseat, and the car drove away, heading west.

About an hour later, several witnesses saw the maroon sedan driving up the hill on Dutch Canyon Road just west of Scappoose. The big car was full of people as it went up the hill slowly. A little while later, several residents of the farming community heard gunshots in the hills. Gunfire was common in the hills around Scappoose, a popular hunting site, so no one paid it any attention. A few people saw the big maroon car driving much faster down the hill a few minutes later. The next morning, L.W. Morgan, driving up Dutch Canyon Road to his small logging operation, found the bullet-riddled bodies of Jimmy Walker and Edith McClain.

"GANGSTERS SLAY 2 NEAR PORTLAND"
Oregonian, April 23, 1933

Police Chief Leon Jenkins assumed that the "gangland" killing was linked with the shooting of Frank Kodat, so police began to round up Kodat's friends, starting with Abe Levine, who had been out of jail for less than twenty-four hours. Jake Silverman was taken into custody and identified as the driver of the sedan by witnesses. They found Mrs. Silverman's Studebaker at a garage on Southeast Belmont and seized it just before garage attendants could switch the new tires on it for a worn-out old pair, as Silverman's brother, Morris, had requested that morning. The tires matched prints left in the mud at the murder scene.

Ed Francisco "Frisco" Burke was wearing a wine-colored suit similar to the one described by witnesses when he was arrested. Some of Kodat's friends, such as Robert "Baby" Burns, seemed to want to be arrested. Burns, who had recently been released from Oregon State Penitentiary after serving ten years for armed robbery, showed up at the city jail and asked to visit Abe Levine. Guards found a loaded revolver and a whole box of bullets in his pocket. Under interrogation, he confessed to four armed robberies that had occurred in the last two days. In all, twenty-seven people were arrested, most of them ex-convicts or their girlfriends, and most of them were held as either suspects or material witnesses for more than a week.

Jack Crim was arrested at a speakeasy on Southwest Montgomery Drive owned by one of his girlfriends, Betty Lamoureaux. He didn't have an alibi for the night of the killing, and a bloodstained suit was found in his hotel room. Even worse, Edith McClain's purse was found in his room, and he was carrying Shy Frank's gun. Crim laughed off the charges, claiming that the blood came from a fight at Lamoureaux's beer garden, where he worked as a bouncer. He said that he picked up the purse at Kodat's when he got the gun. McClain's purse included her birth certificate, several school certificates and a small collection of personal photographs; it was not the kind of thing that she would have left behind.

Just like everyone else involved with the Walker-McClain murders, Jack Crim had spent a few years in the Oregon State Penitentiary for assault with a deadly weapon, committed in Klamath Falls in 1925. Recently, he had started a boxing career as part of Tex Salkeld's lineup of boxers. Salkeld, who eventually became the leading boxing promoter in the Pacific Northwest before his death in 1956, was promoting a popular group of boxers who all took pride in their ethnic identities. Crim was his Indian boxer, often known as the "half breed." Salkeld had several African American boxers, a Filipino, a Chinese and a few other boxers. Through capitalizing on ethnic identities, Salkeld developed a very loyal group of fans, each rooting for his favorite boxer.

All of the suspects and witnesses, except Roy Moore and "Baby" Burns, stonewalled the police, and the only one who faced charges was Jake Silverman, who was charged with first-degree murder. He was tried by Columbia County, where the murders occurred, and the trial was held in Saint Helens. Portland police and the Multnomah County district attorney's office supported the prosecution. Evidence was a little thin. Silverman was convicted of manslaughter and sentenced to three years. He was released from prison in 1936 and returned to Portland, where he ran a tavern, most likely with prostitutes, until his death from a heart attack in 1949.

Frank Kodat, who was probably paying "smile money" to the police, survived his wounds and continued to run his speakeasy and burglary ring until 1942, when he went back to prison on illegal alcohol charges. Abe Levine was already there, after being convicted of the robbery of another clothing store in 1940. Jack Crim enjoyed popularity as the half-breed boxer for several years before he was arrested for violence during a labor strike in 1938. Crim was a goon in the Teamsters organization that was trying to move in on the Portland rackets. By the end of World War II, Crim had returned to Portland and made a reputation for himself as a boxing trainer.

With the coming of the New Deal, the worst days of the Great Depression were in the past, but it would be a decade before hard times had truly passed. In the meantime, organized crime grew in power and scope in Portland. *Photograph by Ralph Eddy. Courtesy of oldoregonphotos.com.*

By the time Shy Frank went to jail for the last time, people like James "Big Jim" Elkins had begun to take over the smaller organizations in an attempt to control Portland's criminal enterprises. Elkins's operation self-destructed in the 1950s from his attempts to stop the Seattle Teamsters from taking over in what came to be known as the "Portland Vice Scandal." From time to time, large national criminal syndicates attempted to gain control over crime in Portland, but they were usually stopped by well-organized local groups.

The Other Side, 1945

A frican Americans have been part of Oregon's history since Marcus
Lopez stepped onto the beach at Tillamook Bay in 1788. Abner and
Lynda Francis were pioneer black Portlanders who gathered signatures from
225 of their neighbors in their effort to overturn the Black Exclusion Law that
was passed in 1851. The law wasn't repealed until 1854, but they stayed in
Portland and ran a popular dry goods store specializing in fabrics near Third
and Morrison. In 1857, the *Oregonian* referred to Mr. Francis as a "black man
and a good citizen." Further Black Exclusion laws and local "sundown" laws
discouraged migration of African Americans to Oregon, but they usually
exempted those who currently lived in the state, so there was always a small
black community. In 1874, when the railroad arrived in Portland, steady jobs
for African Americans were available for the first time, and Portland became
the center of the black community in the state.

Following the example of the Francis family, the African American
community in Portland has always been politically active. In 1867, the black
community, fewer than two hundred strong in a city of seven thousand and
excluded from the Portland public schools, forced the city to give its members
tax rebates so they could open the Portland Colored School. The experiment
taught Portlanders the expense of public education, and as cheap Portlanders
usually do, they took the least expensive solution and integrated the public
schools in 1873. The political cohesion of the black community in Portland
gave them strength beyond their numbers. The availability of decent jobs with
the railroad, hotels and restaurants in the city provided the basis for a black
middle class. Black-owned businesses sprang up to supply their needs, which
encouraged the growth of the community. In 1894, the New Port Republican

In 1941, the *Star of Oregon*, Henry Kaiser's first Liberty ship, was launched. Shipbuilding stimulated incredible growth in Portland's population. *Courtesy of oldoregonphotos.com.*

Club, organized by the waiters at the Portland Hotel, brought pressure on the city Police Bureau, and two black officers were hired. George Hardin, one of the two, kept his job until 1915, when he became the first black Multnomah County deputy, serving until the 1930s.

In 1880, the population of African Americans in Portland reached about 1,100 and remained stable for the next twenty-five years. Most black Portlanders lived close to the railroad station in Northwest Portland. In 1906, the Golden West Hotel on Northwest Third and Elliott opened and became the geographic center of the black community. Before 1919, African Americans could and did rent or own property anywhere in the city. That year, the Portland Realty Board added a provision to its code of ethics that barred realtors from selling property to blacks or Asians in predominantly white neighborhoods. This was the beginning of the segregated housing policies that concentrated the black community into the neighborhood on the east side of the Broadway Bridge, centered on the intersection of Northeast Williams and Weidler Streets, where the Rose Quarter is today.

European American Portlanders, unlike residents of the rest of the state, were usually accepting of African Americans as long as they "knew their place." This patronizing attitude, although highly frustrating for individuals, has allowed opportunities for the group. The early decades of the twentieth century were a prosperous time for the black citizens of Portland, and a vibrant community grew. By the end of the 1920s, there were about two thousand African American Portlanders. The European American population changed significantly during that time as immigration from Europe brought in a wide variety of ethnic groups. At the start of the twentieth century, more than half of Portland's population was born overseas.

Many of these immigrants were looked down on by the predominantly Anglo-Saxon and Protestant older citizens. Response to ethnic discrimination increased the importance of a "white" identity, and anti-black prejudice grew. A system of segregation, referred to as the "Color Line," came into being that restricted black access to public accommodations such as theaters and restaurants. The Ku Klux Klan became politically powerful in the state in the early 1920s, but in Oregon, the members saved their hatred and violence mostly for Catholics and labor organizers. In fact, in 1912, a local Portland KKK klavern donated the lumber to build the new Mount Olivet Baptist Church at Northeast Schuyler and First. Mount Olivet Baptist became one of the most politically active and influential African American churches in the city.

In reaction to the increasing resistance to black civil rights, Portland African Americans organized. In 1903, *The Advocate*, under the editorship of E.D. Cannaday, began publication. In 1912, Beatrice Cannaday, the editor's wife, joined the paper's staff and took over daily operations. Mrs. Cannaday, Oregon's first black female attorney, was a powerful community organizer, and in 1914, she gained an important group of allies when she became founding secretary of the city's National Association for the Advancement of Colored People (NAACP) chapter. Even Beatrice Cannaday, irrepressible community activist that she was, became discouraged during the Great Depression. Economic hard times hit Portland, but they hit none harder than African American Portlanders. As jobs disappeared, the black-owned businesses supported by those salaries went out of business. In 1930, the Golden West itself closed its doors, and the exodus to the east side was pretty much complete.

World War II brought great changes to Portland, as it did to the rest of the country. In Portland, the new Kaiser Shipyards created a multitude of jobs and a severe labor shortage. Kaiser recruited workers, black and white, from all parts of the country, and Portland's population grew by a factor of ten. The African American population grew from about two thousand in 1940 to

Portland resisted public housing until the city was bursting at the seams. The Guilds Lake Housing Project was one of the few areas where African Americans were allowed to buy or rent homes. *Courtesy of Portland City Archives.*

more than twenty thousand by 1943. The majority of new black Portlanders came from east Texas and Louisiana. Moving north, they thought they were coming to a land of freedom, but they were disappointed to see "White Trade Only" signs in Portland restaurants and public facilities. Most of the new white Portlanders were from the South as well, and they faced nearly as much discrimination as the black southerners did. In the European American and African American communities, a split developed between the old Portlanders and the newcomers. Most of the old Portlanders hoped that when the war was over, the newcomers would go back where they came from.

Housing, always at a premium in Portland, was in seriously short supply for all of the newcomers, but the shortage was especially dire for the new African American Portlanders, who were restricted to buying and renting in the northeast Portland neighborhood that came to be known as "Black Broadway," "Colored Town" or the "Other Side." By the end of 1941, most of the black newcomers in Portland were crowded into the crumbling old houses along and near Williams Avenue, living in converted attics or renting couches and beds in overcrowded houses. "The Avenue," as Williams was called, developed as the most exciting neighborhood in town when it came to entertainment. Jazz clubs, like the famous Dude Ranch, sprang up, and talented local jazz musicians were joined by national acts such as Charlie Barnet, Nat King Cole and Billie Holiday. The shipyards worked around-the-clock shifts, and soon midnight on the Avenue was the main part of the day.

Portland, a city founded by real estate developers, resisted the notion of affordable housing from the start. Unwilling to weaken rents and property values or to provide permanent housing for what they hoped was a temporary population increase, Portlanders refused over and over to accept public housing as an option. In 1941, with huge demand for shipping caused by the naval war in the North Atlantic, the first Kaiser Shipyard opened in Portland and began producing Liberty Ships. By the time Pearl Harbor was bombed in December, Kaiser had imported more than 2,500 workers to the area, about 300 of them African American. On December 12, 1941, the Housing Authority of Portland (HAP) was formed with the mission to deal with the housing shortage. HAP, dominated by realtors, served more as an obstacle to the development of housing than a facilitator, though. The main HAP projects were dormitories in strategic neighborhoods; each project faced intense opposition from residents of the neighborhoods.

In the summer of 1942, with two more shipyards ready to open and shantytowns in Sullivan's Gulch, the east side of the Ross Island Bridge and along Interstate Avenue bursting at the seams, Henry Kaiser took action. Kaiser purchased 650 acres of land at the top of the Willamette peninsula, on the delta where the Willamette enters the Columbia River, and just outside of the Portland city limit. Kaiser never thought small, and his original plan was to build six thousand housing units and all of the necessary support facilities on the land. The number of units was soon raised to ten thousand. Kaiser was also famous for working fast. On August 21, 1942, five thousand workers began laying foundations in what was at first called Kaiserville. By December, more than seven hundred housing units had been completed, and the first residents had moved into the new city of Vanport. In less than a year, the country's largest housing project and Oregon's second-largest city was conceived, planned and built.

Community leaders, such as J. James Clow, pastor of the Mount Olivet Baptist Church, called for open housing policies, but HAP was nothing if not segregationist. Dominated by realtors who felt it was part of their ethical code to enforce housing segregation, HAP restricted African American housing to specific neighborhoods in Vanport and in the new Guilds Lake Housing Project, built by the federal government in Northwest Portland. Racial segregation in public housing promoted crowding and all of the social problems that go with it. Incidents of juvenile delinquency and street crime grew, and it became a frequent occurrence for people to be robbed at gunpoint on the street. Many Portlanders felt that the increased number of African Americans in the city was the cause of the increase in crime, but the truth is that most of the people

6/15/48 AERIAL VIEW FLOOD WATERS
Vanport area East from N. Denver Ave.

Vanport, the other housing project that allowed African American residents, was devastated by a flood in 1948. *Courtesy of Portland City Archives.*

involved turned out to be soldiers from Swan Island or Vancouver Barracks or airmen from the Portland Air Field—and almost all of them were white.

In 1945, with the war winding down, Portland felt it was done with the whole project of public housing and began to tear down housing units in Guilds Lake and Vanport. Some of the new workers began to move out of the area as many of the jobs in the shipyard ended, but many of them stayed. As units went down and the white population fled, the percentage of African Americans in Vanport and Guilds Lake increased. The apartments and duplexes that had sprung up during the war were built quickly with cheap materials; they had not been built to last. The African Americans who remained in these neighborhoods lived in shabby, crowded conditions. Many of them facing unemployment started to become desperate for a way to support themselves. Easy access to firearms and alcohol led to some serious outbursts of violence.

"2 Negroes Die, 1 in Jail in Guilds Lake Flareup"
Oregonian, August 22, 1945

Three homicides in 1945, one in Vanport and two in Guild's Lake, were very important to the development of the African American community in Portland.

The first killing took place in August. The second followed immediately as a result of the first. Beatrice Terry, thirty-five, moved to Portland from Los Angeles early in 1944 to work in the shipyards. While in Los Angeles, she had been shot and nearly killed by a violent ex-lover named Scott E. Thomas. Thomas, who had a history of violence against women, felt that if he couldn't have Terry, no one would. In 1945, Thomas moved into the Guilds Lake Housing Project, just a few blocks down Northwest Forty-first Avenue from Beatrice Terry.

There is no record of their meeting, or whether Terry knew he was there, but Thomas probably saw her at some point with another man. On the night of August 21, 1945, Scott Thomas asked his friend Cliff Blivens to help him get a gun and give him a ride. Blivens probably took his friend down to Williams Avenue, where vice lord Tom Johnson ruled and booze and guns were cheap. They drove back to Guilds Lake, and Blivens dropped Thomas off in front of Terry's house. Shortly before 11:00 p.m., Blivens was turning his car around to head for home when he heard two gunshots. Frightened, he took off before Thomas came back out, but two other witnesses saw him come out of Terry's apartment. When they investigated, they found Beatrice Terry dead.

The Guilds Lake Project, unlike Vanport, was within the Portland city limits, so Portland detective Sergeant Dan Mitola responded to the shooting with Detectives Mike O'Leary and Bard Purcell. The Portland Police Bureau was at the beginning of an era that has become known as the "Smile Money" period; graft from illegal gambling, drinking and prostitution was prevalent, and police autonomy was at a high point. Police officers, who could collect $200 to $500 ($2,400 to $6,100 in 2013) per week from graft, were able to sustain a privileged lifestyle, and they felt privileged to do what they wanted on the job as well. The city's response to rising crime rates promoted autonomy of the police and violence. In 1945, the Police Bureau started running "shotgun squads" through certain neighborhoods from midnight to dawn. Tactics such as this led to tension between the police and residents, and confrontations sometimes turned violent.

Relations between the police and the African American community were tense. The Police Bureau, like the Multnomah County Sheriff's Department that policed Vanport, was sensitive to the issue of race, and it took many experimental steps in improving community relations. In Guilds Lake, the Portland Police Bureau organized a Junior Police League in which officers worked with children in the housing project. The Junior Police League was integrated and had quite a bit of support from the African American community. Black officers were assigned to police African American neighborhoods as much as possible, but there were no black detectives to respond to major crimes such as homicide.

Some of the African American officers, such as Deputies Matt Dishman and Bill Travis, became community leaders and had positive impact on the relationship between their department and citizens. Others, like Deputy Sam Blanchard, as corrupt and abusive as the worst white cop, did just the opposite.

Murder policing in a Portland black neighborhood in 1945 meant that anyone on the street was immediately arrested for interrogation. Two witnesses identified Scott Thomas as the man with the gun. At least one witness led the police to Cliff Blivens, who was interrogated and held as a material witness. Detective Sergeant Mitola and Deputy District Attorney John R. Collier quickly organized a manhunt. Purcell and O'Leary began raiding hotels and rooming houses along Williams Avenue looking for Thomas. At about 2:00 a.m., Purcell and O'Leary spoke with a Guilds Lake neighborhood character named General Grant, who had a history of accusing his neighbors of crimes. Grant told the police that Thomas had been in the house of Grant's neighbor, Ervin Jones.

Ervin Jones, originally from Louisiana, lived with his wife and two children, as well as his wife's two sisters and two brothers in a two-bedroom duplex apartment on Northwest Forty-fourth Court in Guilds Lake. Ervin and his two brothers-in-law worked at one of the shipyards. The two brothers were at work that night; everyone else had gone to bed by the time the police arrived to check on Grant's accusation. Thinking they were hot on Thomas's trail, Sergeant Mitola and D.A. Collier accompanied the two detectives to the Jones home. The cul-de-sac design of the Guilds Lake Project oriented the houses with their backs toward the street, so Mitola, O'Leary and Collier approached the back door while Purcell went around to cover the front with a shotgun.

Elva Jones woke up when her husband got out of bed and shouted, "Who knocks?" As he walked out of the bedroom, she heard glass breaking near the back door. Ervin pounded on the wall in the hallway, yelling, "Wake up! Robbers breaking in!" His wife, her sisters and their children cowered behind the bed, while Ervin walked toward the back door, loading his handgun. The police had begun pounding on the back door. Jesse Johnson, who lived in the adjoining unit, opened his door, and Sergeant Mitola pointed his pistol at him and ordered him to get back inside. Detective Purcell was watching through a window near the front door as Ervin Jones emerged from the hallway and turned toward the back door. Purcell stuck the barrel of his shotgun through the window and yelled, "Lay that damn gun down or I'll blow out your brains."

Purcell claimed that Jones fired two shots at the back door and was turning toward him before he fired, but there is no evidence that Jones even got his gun loaded. He was dead before he hit the floor. It soon became evident that

Thomas was not at the Jones residence and never had been. Ervin Jones had no connection to the case at all; his death had been a terrible accident. Captain James Fleming, chief of detectives, ruled that the shooting had been justified, and Detective Purcell remained on duty. Thomas was arrested early the next morning near Northwest Fourth and Glisan. He admitted the shooting, saying, "I shot her once before and this time I really meant business."

Detective John Bardell "Bard" Purcell had been a star athlete at Linfield College before joining the Portland Police Bureau in 1940. His brother, James, had been on the force for two years, and both of them rose through the ranks quickly. The Purcell brothers, natives of The Dalles, were descendants of Edward Crate, a pioneer of Wasco County whose four sons all served as policemen in The Dalles and Portland. They were both hired as part of Police Chief Harry Niles's efforts to improve the education of officers in the Portland Police Bureau, and they were part of what most officers called "Niles' college boys." James Purcell, the older brother, would become Portland police chief in 1953 but would be indicted and forced to resign in 1957 during the "Portland Vice Scandal." The shooting of Ervin Jones would slow Bard Purcell's advancement slightly, but he would continue to rise up the ranks in a career that spanned more than thirty years, eventually becoming a captain and then Multnomah County sheriff.

It took a few days, but soon the outcry from the community was loud over Jones's death. Reverend J. James Clow of Mount Olivet Baptist Church called for an investigation into the shooting, and Irvin Goodman, one of Portland's most famous attorneys, agreed to represent the Jones family. Elva Jones had taken her children and sisters back to Louisiana after her husband's death, and raising money for her to return to Portland for an investigation became a major organizing tool. Because of community pressure, there would be two investigations into the Jones shooting; a coroner's inquest and a Multnomah County Grand Jury investigation. Both would rule that Jones died by justifiable homicide.

Dr. Denorval Unthank, Portland's most prestigious African American doctor, donated office space and organized the community to hire Edwin "Bill" Berry from Chicago to head a Portland chapter of the Urban League. Berry was a talented organizer, and with the support of Unthank, Reverend Clow and Irvin Goodwin the new Urban League took the lead in organizing around the Jones shooting and the execution of Wardell Henderson in 1948. These issues, in conjunction with the aggressive work of E. Shelton "Shelly" Hill, the Urban League's job developer, led to a period of intense political activism around civil rights issues in Portland.

Until the day the levee broke, Portland announced that there was no danger of flooding in Vanport. The city's negligence and reluctance to admit casualties fed the distrust that pervaded the African American community. *Photograph by Allen DeLay.* ©*Tom Robinson.*

Wardell Henderson served with the United States Sixth Army, headquartered at the Presidio of San Francisco. The Sixth Army participated in the liberation of New Guinea and the Philippines and was scheduled to participate in the invasion of Japan before the Japanese surrender. Henderson had a good record during the war, rising to the rank of sergeant, but for some reason he went AWOL in March 1945 from the Presidio of San Francisco and came to Portland with his wife, who was from Yelm, Washington. Henderson's wife took a job in the shipyards, but Henderson, using the alias Aaron Robinson, kept a low profile and spent his time drinking and gambling.

On Christmas Eve 1945, Wardell Henderson drank a bottle of whiskey, took a gun he had bought a few days before and went looking for Jerry Taylor, a man who owed him money and had been avoiding him. Henderson found Taylor and another man at Taylor's apartment in Vanport. There was a loud argument, and Henderson fired several shots, hitting Taylor in the groin but not killing him. The other man jumped out a window and ran away. Henderson didn't get his money, and he was highly agitated when he got back to his own apartment. He told his wife about the shooting and said he had to get out of town.

"Butcher Found Shot to Death"
Oregonian, December 26, 1945

Walter Poole, thirty-nine, lived in Vancouver and worked as a butcher at the Jantzen Beach Food Market. On Christmas Eve, he worked the evening shift from 4:00 p.m. to 11:00 p.m. After work, there was a small Christmas party, and the store manager handed out $20 bills as a Christmas bonus. It was almost midnight when Poole left the store and walked toward his car, a blue 1940 Chevy that was parked nearby. He was carrying nearly $200 ($2,100 in 2013) in his wallet. Someone accosted Poole near his car and forced him to drive to Vanport, a short distance in the opposite direction from Poole's home.

Poole's body was found on Christmas Day in front of a partially dismantled apartment complex. He had been badly beaten and shot in the back. His wallet, watch and ring were missing, but he still had his twenty-dollar Christmas bonus in his shirt pocket. Poole's car was seen in a downtown Portland garage that day, having the clutch repaired. It was driven by Aaron Robinson, who was accompanied by a white soldier. The car was found a few days later, broken down outside Cedar Rapids, Iowa. A nationwide search began for Aaron Robinson, but there was no trace of him.

Wardell Henderson arrived in Philadelphia a few days later and spent a few days at his mother's home. The next day, he surrendered to military authorities on AWOL charges. Two Portland detectives went to Philadelphia and interrogated Henderson about the Poole murder. Henderson claimed that he had been drunk on Christmas Eve and admitted to the shooting of Jerry Taylor. He said he couldn't remember anything about Walter Poole, but he was wearing the dead man's ring. Under intense interrogation Henderson admitted the killing, claiming that the gun went off accidently, and he was returned to Portland to face a charge of first-degree murder.

Henderson was convicted, based on circumstantial evidence, in a trial that played on Portland's fears. One of the jurors, quoted in an affidavit that was part of Henderson's appeal, said, "An example must be made of a Negro…or they will overrun us." It is difficult to tell more than sixty years later whether Henderson was actually guilty. It was a point of faith among African Americans and their supporters that he was not. As his execution approached, organizing

The Vanport and Guilds Lake Housing Projects consisted of temporary structures built with shoddy materials never meant to last. The flood in 1948 was completely devastating to Vanport. Many hoped that the African American population would leave the city. Fortunately, they were disappointed. *Courtesy of Portland City Archives.*

became very intense, and the groundwork was laid for a strong civil rights movement in Portland.

There was nothing they could do to save Henderson, and he was executed by gas chamber in January 1948. His death was an issue that galvanized the movement and greatly bolstered its organization. The Urban League, taking advantage of the larger African American population, established itself in Portland as a force to be reckoned with. When Vanport was destroyed in a flood a few months later, the organization was already in place to strongly challenge Portland's segregated housing and public facility policies. It took more than two decades of intense organizing to begin to enforce civil rights for blacks in Portland, but the tradition of political activism and the increased black population were used to good effect. The distrust the African American community felt for the city government after the Vanport flood was a legacy of occurrences such as the Ervin Jones and Wardell Henderson killings.

Bibliography

The basic facts and stories in this book are based on close readings of the *Portland Oregonian* and other daily and weekly newspapers from Portland, Oregon. This information is catalogued in my larger project the "Slabtown Chronology." The interpretations and opinions expressed are my own. The following resources were helpful in forming these opinions and interpretations.

Alborn, Denise M. "Crimping and Shanghaiing on the Columbia River." *Oregon Historical Quarterly* 93, no. 3. (Fall 1992): 262–91.

Beck, Dana. "Roy Clifford's Life in Groceries—and Memories of the Clifford Family." *Sellwood Bee.* www.readthebee.com/community.html.

Bigelow, William, and Diamond, Norman. "Agitate, Educate, Organize: Portland, 1934." *Oregon Historical Quarterly* 89, no. 1 (Spring 1988): 4–29.

Blalock, Barney. *Portland's Lost Waterfront.* Charleston, SC: The History Press, 2012.

Boag, Peter. *Same Sex Affairs: Constructing and Controlling Homosexuality in the Pacific Northwest.* Berkeley: University of California Press, 2003.

Booth, Brian. *Wildmen, Wobblies and Whistle Punks: Stewart Holbrook's Lowbrow Northwest.* Corvallis: Oregon State University Press, 1992.

Bottenberg, Ray, and Jeanna Bottenberg. *Vanishing Portland.* Charleston, SC: Arcadia Publishing, 2008.

Burchill, John. "The Strangler." Winnipeg Police Service. www.winnipeg.ca/police/history/story21.stm.

Chinese in Northwest America Research Committee. www.cinarc.org.

Cohen, Patricia C. "The Helen Jewett Murder: Violence, Gender and Sexual Licentiousness in Antebellum America." *NWSA Journal* 2, no. 3 (Summer 1990): 374–89.

De Lorme, Roland L. "Crime and Punishment in the Pacific Northwest Territories: A Bibliographic Essay." *Pacific Northwest Quarterly* 76, no. 2 (April 1985): 42–51.

Bibliography

Dietsch, Robert. *Jumptown: The Golden Years of Portland Jazz, 1942–1957.* Corvallis: Oregon State University Press, 2005.

Donnely, Robert C. "Organizing Portland: Organized Crime, Municipal Corruption and the Teamster's Union." *Oregon Historical Quarterly*, 104, no. 3 (Fall 2003): 334–65.

Field, Peter. "Dolly Adams, the Water Queen." *Guidelines Newsletter*, 2012. http://www.sfcityguides.org/public_guidelines.html?srch_text=Dolly+Adams%2C+the+Water+Queen&submit=Search&submitted2=TRUE.

Foster, Doug. "Imperfect Justice: The Modoc War Crimes Trial of 1873." *Oregon Historical Quarterly* 100, no. 3 (Fall 1999): 246–87.

Fryer, Heather. "Race, Industry and the Aesthetic of a Changing Community in World War II Portland." *Pacific Northwest Quarterly* 96, no. 1 (Winter 2004/2005): 3–13.

Gaston, Joseph. *Portland, Oregon: Its History and Builders.* Chicago: S.J. Clark Publishing Company, 1911.

Gibbens, Mark. "Earle Leonard Nelson: The Dark Strangler." CrimeLibrary, 2011. www.trutv.com/library/crime/serial_killers/history/earle_nelson/17.html.

Goldstein, Leslie F. "Popular Sovereignty, the Origins of Judicial Review, and the Revival of the Unwritten Law." *The Journal of Politics* 48, no. 1 (February 1986): 51–71.

Hoffman, Dennis E., and Webb, Vincent J. "Police Response to Labor Radicalism in Portland and Seattle 1913–1919." *Oregon Historical Quarterly* 87, no, 4 (Winter 1986): 341–66.

Horowitz, David A. "Social Morality and Personal Revitalization: Oregon's Ku Klux Klan in the 1920s." *Oregon Historical Quarterly* 90, no. 4 (Winter 1989): 365–84.

Hunt, Dana E. "Drugs and Consensual Crimes: Drug Dealing and Prostitution." *Crime and Justice* 13 (1990): 159–202.

Ireland, Robert M. "Insanity and the Unwritten Law." *American Journal of Legal History* 32, no. 2 (April 1988): 157–72.

John, Finn J.D. *Wicked Portland: The Wild and Lusty Underworld of a Frontier Seaport Town.* Charleston, SC: The History Press, 2012.

Johnston, Robert D. "The Myth of the Harmonious City: Will Daly, Lora Little and the Hidden Face of Progressive Era Portland." *Oregon Historical Quarterly* 99, no. 3 (Fall 1998): 248–97.

Kelley, Joseph. *Thirteen Years in the Oregon Penitentiary.* [Portland, OR?] Obtained from GoogleBooks, 1908.

Lansing, Robert B. "The Tragedy of Charity Lamb, Oregon's First Convicted Murderess." *Oregon Historical Quarterly* 101, no. 1 (Spring 2000): 40–76.

Leeson, Fred. *Rose City Justice: A Legal History of Portland, Oregon.* Portland: Oregon Historical Society Press, 1998.

Leo, Richard A. *Police Interrogation and American Justice.* Cambridge, MA: Harvard University Press, 2009. Obtained from GoogleBooks. http://books.google.com/books?id=D6J2jTOXCUMC&dq=interrogation+nineteenth+century&source=gbs_navlinks_s.

MacColl, E. Kimbark, with Harry Stein. *Merchants, Money and Power: The Portland Establishment, 1843–1913.* Portland, OR: Georgian Press, 1988.

Mass, Ernest B. "Election Poster Details," 1911. Old Oregon Photos. www.oldoregonphotos.com/location/oregoncounties/clackamas-county/sheriff-ernest-t-mass-election-poster.html.

McElderry, Stuart. "Building a West Coast Ghetto: African-American Housing in Portland 1910–1960." *Pacific Northwest Quarterly* 92, no. 3 (Summer 2001): 137–48.

———. "Vanport Conspiracy Rumors and Social Relations in Portland 1940–1950." *Oregon Historical Quarterly* 99, no. 2 (Summer 1998): 134–63.

Munk, Michael. *Portland Red Guide.* 2nd ed. Portland, OR: Ooligan Press, 2011.

———. "Portland's Silk Stocking Mob: The Citizen Emergency League in the 1934 Maritime Strike." *Pacific Northwest Quarterly* 91, no. 3 (Summer 2000): 150–60.

Murell, Gary. "Hunting Reds in Oregon, 1935–1939." *Oregon Historical Quarterly* 100, no. 4 (Winter 1999): 374–401.

Nelson, Bruce. "Unions and the Popular Front: The West Coast Waterfront in the 1930s." *International Labor and Working Class History*, no. 30 (Fall 1986): 56–78.

Nelson, Donald. *A Pictorial History of St. Johns.* Portland, OR: D. Nelson Books, 2011.

Off Our Backs 16, no. 8. "Domestic Violence: A Crime Is a Crime" (August/September 1986): 9.

Olsen, Polina. *Stories from Jewish Portland.* Charleston, SC: The History Press, 2011.

Oregon History Project. "John H. Mitchell," 2002. www.ohs.org/education/oregonhistory/Oregon-Biographies-John-Mitchell.cfm.

Pearson, Rudy. "A Menace to the Neighborhood: Housing and African Americans in Portland 1941–1945." *Oregon Historical Quarterly* 102, no. 2 (Summer 2010): 158–79.

Pitzer, Paul C. "Dorothy McCullough Lee: The Successes and Failures of Dottie-Do-Good." *Oregon Historical Quarterly* 91, no. 1 (Spring 1990): 4–42.

Polk's Portland City Directories. Multnomah County Library. Portland, Oregon.

Portland Bureau of Planning. *History of Portland's African-American Community (1805–Present).* City of Portland, Oregon, 1993.

Recker, Yvonne. (2002). "According to Madelaine Bohl…" Message on Rootsweb ORFORUM. http://archiver.rootsweb.ancestry.com/th/read/ORFORUM/2002-12/1039380705.

Richard, K. Kieth. "Unwelcome Settlers: Black and Mulatto Oregon Pioneers." *Oregon Historical Quarterly* 84, nos. 1 and 2 (Spring/Summer 1983): 29–55; 173–205.

Robinson, William. "Oregon in Depression and War." Oregon History Project, 2002. www.ohs.org/education/oregonhistory/narratives/subtopic.cfm?subtopic_id=102.

Safford, Jeffrey J. "The Pacific Coast Maritime Strike of 1936: Another View." *Pacific Historical Review* 77, no. 4 (November 2008): 585–615.

Smith, Georgia. "Shanghaiing." FoundSF. http://foundsf.org/index.php?title=Shanghaiing.

Snyder, Eugene. *Portland Names and Neighborhoods: Their Historic Origins.* Portland, OR: Binford and Mort, 1979.

Taylor, Qunitard. "The Great Migration: The Afro-American Communities of Seattle and Portland during the 1940s." *Arizona and the West* 23, no. 2 (Summer 1981): 109–26.

Thompson, Richard. *Portland's Streetcars.* Charleston, SC: Arcadia Publishing, 2006.

Tracy, Charles. "A Historical Perspective on Race and Crime: Chinese Arrests in Portland, Oregon 1871–1885." Unpublished thesis, 1980. Courtesy of Portland Police Historical Society.

———. "Police Function in Portland, 1851–1874." *Oregon Historical Quarterly* 80, nos. 1, 2 and 3 (Spring/Summer/Fall 1979).

———. Unpublished James Lappeus research, 1983. Courtesy of Portland Police Museum.

Tyler, Robert L. "I.W.W. in the Pacific N.W.: Rebels of the Woods." *Oregon Historical Quarterly* 55, no. 1 (March 1954): 3–44.

Udall, Stewart, Robert Dykstra, Michael Bellesiles, Paula Marks and Gregory Nobles. "How the West Got Wild: American Media and Frontier Violence—A Roundtable." *Western Historical Quarterly* 31, no. 3 (Autumn 2000): 277–95.

Uruburu, Paula. *American Eve: Evelyn Nesbit, Stanford White, the Birth of the IT Girl and the Crime of the Century.* New York: Riverhead Books, 2008.

U.S. Census, Portland, Multnomah, Oregon, 1880. Roll 1083, film 1255083, page 256B, Enumeration District 095, image 0095. Ancestry.com.

Vance, Rupert B., and Waller Wynn Jr. "Folk Rationalizations in the Unwritten Law." *American Journal of Sociology* 39, no. 4 (January 1934): 483–92.

Willing, Joseph K. "The Profession of Bootlegging." *Annals of the American Academy of Political and Social Sciences* 125 (May 1926): 40–48.

Index

About the Author

JD Chandler is a former political/labor activist and currently a public historian specializing in the history of crime in Portland. During the last sixteen years, he has been making a study of murder in Portland and compiling the "Slabtown Chronology." Up to this time, his work has been published online through his "Slabtown Chronicle" blog (www.portlandcrime. blogspot.com). He has been writing  fiction and nonfiction his whole life, but in the last few years, criminal history has been his main focus. He currently blogs on Portland's weird history on his "Weird Portland" blog (www.weirdportland.blogspot.com).

CPSIA information can be obtained
at www.ICGtesting.com
Printed in the USA
LVHW081905281222
735983LV00003B/174